# My 60s & Childhood

## A Memoir

## *Rain McAlistair*

**Ireland 2015**

© 2015 Rain McAlistair

*All rights reserved*

*This book is a memoir.
I have tried to recreate events, locales and conversations from my memories of them. In order to maintain their anonymity in some instances I have changed the names of individuals and places, I may have changed some identifying characteristics and details such as physical properties, occupations and places of residence.*

*Front Cover Design by Kit*

ISBN - 13: 978-1519469793
ISBN- 10: 1519469799

### *This book is dedicated to Mum & Dad*

*"You don't choose your family. They are God's gift to you, as you are to them."*

*- Desmond Tutu*

**Also by Rain McAlistair:**

*Dove (2010)*

*Bridge (2011)*

*Moonchaser (2012)*

*Leaving (2013)*

**Short story collaboration:**

*L is For (2014)*

# 1 ~ HANDING OVER THE PURSE

Nowadays, most people go to the supermarket on a Friday and do a big weekly shop. It wasn't really like that when I was a child. For one thing, we had no car, so all groceries had to be carried home.

There was a row of small shops about half a mile from my home. Like all the other children where I lived, I was sent every day with a shopping bag, a list and a purse to do the family daily shop. (For those overseas from me, by a purse I mean a woman's leather money holder.)

I was so young when I was first entrusted with this important job that I couldn't yet read. This was no problem. My mum would write her shopping list in sections, headed with the name of each shop. Then she would tear the list into strips, with one shop on each strip.

There were thirteen shops: off-license (liquor store,) sweet shop/post office, haberdasher, chemist, butcher, optician, hairdresser, two grocers, ironmonger, toyshop, barber and greengrocer. At the end of the row was a launderette and next to that, a tiny library and a church.

Off I would go, carefully crossing two roads. My first port of call was always the butcher's. I would hand over the bag, strips of paper and purse. The butcher would find the right strip and chop up and weigh the meat accordingly. After taking his payment he would pop the purse and shopping in the bag and hand it over. He would then select another strip, hand it to me and tell me which shop I needed to go to next: 'this one's for the chemist, love.' All of the shopkeepers did the same, destroying their strip after serving me. When I ran out of strips of paper, I knew I had finished and could set off for home.

Different shops had different atmospheres. The butcher's had clean sawdust on the floor. Only men worked there. They were always whistling, singing, laughing and teasing. By contrast, only women worked in the sweet shop/ post office. They were always busy and could be a little stern. My least favourite shop to visit was the ironmonger's. A man and his teenage son worked there. They were very grumpy and neither ever smiled.

I would spend a long time gazing into the toyshop window. It was owned by a wonderful, very tall old gentleman. He had a grey bristle brush moustache and little, round glasses. On Saturdays I would spend my precious two shillings and sixpence pocket money in there. My choice of toy required careful consideration all week.

One day I was sent specifically just to the chemist. My mum handed me an empty bottle which had held sweet, sticky, pink medicine that my sister had been taking for some childhood ailment. I was told to ask the chemist for a refill. I was in a great hurry because I wanted to get back and play, so I grabbed a plastic carrier bag from the glory hole (a cupboard under the stairs that held everything) and ran all the way.

'My sister is ill and has been taking this. Mum says can we have it refilled please?' I thrust my hand into the bag and pulled out the bottle. My mouth fell open. Something strange had happened to the bottle on the way to the shops. The lid was now encrusted with what looked like dirt. Other bits of dirt clung to the rest of the bottle. I had no idea how this had happened so I had no idea what to say. The chemist took the bottle from me with wide eyes and marched off.

A moment later she returned and handed me a brand new bottle of medicine. Looking at me very hard, she said, 'tell your mother I'm not surprised your sister isn't better as that bottle was filthy! Tell her to keep this one SOMEWHERE CLEAN!' The last two words were emphasised as she leaned closer. Red faced, I nodded and fled.

Outside the shop, I saw there was loose soil in the bag so I carried the medicine in my hand. I had no idea how it had got there but I had a feeling this whole business was going to get me into trouble.

When I told my mum, she immediately realised I had taken a bag which had previously held potatoes. She was hopping mad and so embarrassed that the chemist must now think we lived in a dirty house. Accusations of being less than pristine in one's housekeeping were some of the worst slurs that could be bestowed on anyone.

I was right that I was in big trouble! I always checked the bag before going shopping after that, but I dreaded going into the chemist's for a long time.

## 2 ~ GETTING UP FOR WORK

My dad was a carpenter by trade. He was born in 1919 and served in the Second World War for the whole duration. He moved around a bit after the war working on various projects, including the building of Sellafield Nuclear Power Plant in England which was then called Windscale. Shortly after my birth in 1962, my family moved to a town where factory work was readily available for the men of the area.

I think it was hard for my dad to adjust to factory work. He was no longer required to be creative. His job as a heavy duty machine operator demanded speed and endurance. It was piece work. The building had a glass roof and was very hot in the summer. The noise of the machines was almost overpowering. He worked two alternate weekly shifts. The first was from 6am until 2pm. The second was from 2pm until 10pm. When he got home he always seemed exhausted. He would also be coated in a fine covering of steel dust, which had a very distinctive smell. Sometimes he would get a steel splinter in his eye and would have to go to the local hospital, coming home with an eye patch on. We just accepted this frequent injury as normal.

A lot of fathers in those days were quite distant figures in their children's lives. They worked hard and didn't get involved in child-rearing at all. Us kids were told, 'don't bother your father; he's tired.' I can remember really wanting to show him my latest drawing or whatever but knowing I was not allowed to.

He was one of those men with an extremely heavy, dark beard growth so despite shaving every day, he mostly looked quite severe. If we had been playing my mum up, she sometimes resorted to using the old 'wait till your father gets home' threat to make us behave and on rare occasions we were told off by him. But mostly he didn't get involved.

He cycled to work so he had to get up quite early if he was on the 6 - 2 shift. A strange looking contraption was the thing that ensured he set off on time. It was called a Goblin Teasmade. It was quite big and heavy and made of a sort of yellow/beige Bakelite.

Every night my mum would carry cups, a teapot, tea leaves, milk, sugar and water up to their bedroom and prime this machine to deliver a pot of tea early in the morning. It had a very strong, bare light bulb sticking out of the top. The water would bubble noisily for ages as it heated. Then it was action stations! At the appointed waking up time it would flood the room with light, while an incredibly loud buzzer would wake the whole house in a sort of sleepy panic. The square, silver kettle would then tip up on a kind of hydraulic platform, pouring boiling water into a strategically placed teapot as it went. Many a time my mum forgot to put the teapot there and the boiling water would gush all over their bedside table. But on a good day a pot of tea was ready to aid waking up. It was a very dramatic beginning to the day.

My dad's last act before leaving the house was to put his bicycle clips on. They were metal circles which kept the trouser legs from getting caught in the bicycle chain. He worked at the factory for seventeen years.

The whole routine of the teasmade, the bicycle clips, the smell of the steel dust, the occasional eye patch, the five o clock shadow beard and the exhaustion were all part of how my dad and his working life appeared to me as a child. On his days off, my dad laughed a lot at things like Laurel and Hardy and the comedian Harry Worth making shapes in shop windows on television. But on working days he never smiled. If I could ask him about it now he'd probably just say, 'I wasn't being paid to smile, I was there to work.'

## 3 ~ HONESTY

My generation learned to read from books called the *Janet and John* books. These weren't very exciting stories, and seemed repetitive to me even as a young child. We progressed from *Book One* to *Book Two* and so on, each having a different coloured cover. When you had finished a book you were sent to the head mistress' office to be presented with the next reading book and to receive your reward.

I was a bit scared of our headmistress at my infant school. We rarely had anything to do with her personally but she presided over assembly each day. She had short, tight, curly hair and those glasses that flare out in points at the sides. She reminded me of Meg Richardson from *Crossroads*. After handing in your old book, she would ceremoniously delve into her cupboard and get out her large biscuit tin which was full of Smarties (little candy covered chocolate sweets.) You were allowed to choose one Smartie and eat it there as a reward for completing the book. That's right. One Smartie. It wasn't the biggest incentive in the world.

The teacher would test our reading ability with words from the books printed on small strips of card. We were allowed to take a pile of these words home in little rectangular tins for our parents to test us as homework. We always had to return the tin of words the next day though.

One day I was told to tidy the stock room along with a girl called Jacqueline. Thinking about it now we were a bit little for that job, but we probably did our best to rearrange the things on the bottom shelf. I was quite overawed to be in the stock room because I had never been in there before. My eyes fell onto a pile of empty word tins. Now for some reason I can't explain, I loved little tins and containers.

'I wish I could have one of those of my own,' I sighed longingly. Jacqueline turned to me and smiled.

'Oh but the teacher said we are allowed to take home one each, for tidying the cupboard,' she explained as she stuffed a tin in her pocket.

'Really?' I was delighted and selected a tin for myself.

At home, I carefully placed the tin in pride of place on my dressing table in my bedroom. It had only been there a day when my mum spotted it. She asked me where it came from and I cheerfully told her about Jacqueline saying we could have one each. My mum wasn't buying this and asked the teacher about it the next day.

The upshot was that I was given a very stern lecture by the teacher the next day about stealing.

'You must never, never, NEVER take anything that doesn't belong to you.'

I was really upset and cried more over the telling-off than about the loss of the tin.

When I was about ten the incident of the Sellotape occurred. My sister who was then thirteen had got in with a bit of a bad crowd at school. In the same way that my tin was noticed right away, my mum noticed one day that she had a new large roll of Sellotape in her bedroom. She caved in under questioning and admitted that a friend had stolen it from the local sweet shop and given it to her. If it had been a movie she would have been marched down to the sweet shop to hand it back and say sorry as a lesson to her.

What actually happened was quite strange. All four of us sat down at the living room table and had a family conference about what to do with the stolen goods. My parents were insistent it could not stay in the house. Eventually it was decided we should get rid of it without being seen. I was told to walk down the street with the roll of tape in my pocket and stop at the nearest storm drain. I was instructed to pretend to tie my shoelace and surreptitiously drop the 'hot gear' down the drain.

My heart was thumping as I carried this out. When it was done, I ran back home, very relieved. Three anxious faces peered at me as I came back in.

'Did you do it?'

'Yes.'

It was never mentioned again.

## 4 ~ TRAINS

Young children were given a lot of responsibility by their mums and dads in the sixties and seventies, in a way that would be deemed irresponsible parenting if it went on today. Many of us were latchkey kids, letting ourselves in from school, cooking our own tea and running errands on busy streets when we were practically knee high. We were also left home alone from an early age. Looking back now it was just the done thing in those days. Most children were brought up in the same way. And of course we were cosseted then compared to children who lived half a century before us. They went out to work before reaching their teens. It's all relative.

Having said that, there was one thing my parents did with us kids which looking back even with the benefit of hindsight seems insane. They used to send us 300 miles away on holiday to visit relatives at the other end of Britain, on a train when my sister and I were as young as nine and six respectively... on our own.

The relative at the other end was merely given instructions to meet the train at a certain time. My mum would casually get us seated on the train with our luggage and sandwiches and then would ask the nearest woman to 'keep an eye on them.' Sometimes that woman would get off the train during our journey, usually designating another woman to take over. It was very casual and nobody seemed to see the massive potential for danger or mishap.

What was more, my sister and I would have to change trains halfway. We were told to show our tickets and ask the guard to show us which new train to board. We were often in a state of panic and confusion as we climbed aboard, asking each other 'did he mean this train?' We would always ask a fellow passenger where it was going to be on the safe side.

One day we were on such a trip and after many hours on the trains we arrived at the city of our destination. It was a massive train station. Uncle Bobby was to meet us. We scanned the platform from the train. But there was no Uncle Bobby in sight. We got off and walked up and down the full length of the train, panic rising. Still no Uncle Bobby.

My sister, as the eldest, had been told what to do in this event. Find a telephone box and ring the house we were going to be staying in. She had coins in a special pocket for this emergency, should it arise. My elderly aunt just about had kittens when we phoned, as apparently Uncle Bobby had set off for the station in good time. Our uncle had a heart condition so she was probably just as worried about him as she was about us.

Go back to the platform and ask a guard to wait with us. Those were her instructions. Of course, nobody had mobile phones when this took place so she couldn't phone her husband and say 'where the heck are you?' They didn't have a car and while she was worried, she obviously wasn't worried enough to set off in a taxi for the station herself. She must have been just hoping for the best.

Luckily, about twenty minutes after we had gone back to the platform, Uncle Bobby came rushing up, purple in the face, apologising profusely. He was talking nineteen to the dozen, trying to explain how he had been waiting on the wrong platform. I had seldom seen an adult in such a state of panic.

We took a black cab to their cosy little house and were welcomed by a very relieved and slightly tearful aunt.

They had two cats called Cheeky and Rusty so within a very short time we were playing with them and had almost forgotten our ordeal.

When I grew up, I often shuddered when I thought back to those train journeys. I had thought we were hard done by. But when I was researching my family tree, my dad casually told me that his two very young sisters had been sent to live with a relative abroad. This was because my grandfather had died at the young age of fifty. Dad and his sisters went by boat. He was sent to supervise them and travelled back alone.

I thought for a minute. My grandfather died in 1930. 'So Dad, when this happened; when you took them over on the boat you were only...' I did the maths on my fingers.

'I was eleven,' Dad said. Like I said, it's all relative.

# 5 ~ WINTER

Heating houses fifty years ago was a difficult business as not many folk had central heating. We had an open fire when I was very little and I would run outside to see the chimney sweep's brush poke out the top of the chimney when he came to the house. When I was five, we had a gas fire installed. I was worried about how Santa would get down the chimney with the fire in the way but after that my parents left the back door open for him.

That small gas fire was the only fixed source of heating in the entire house. While we were eating our Reddy Brek before school my mum would sometimes ignite the gas rings on the cooker. This was supposed to take the edge off the cold. In reality it had little effect. Upstairs had no heating at all so paraffin heaters were regularly filled by my dad and carried into various rooms.

The smell wasn't very nice. They were only put in our bedrooms when it was very cold. One day when I was about six, they forgot that they had left a paraffin heater burning in my room. The wick burned completely dry. The fumes were awful and I woke up being carried out by my dad as I coughed and choked.

From a young age I trekked up and down the road to the shops fetching paraffin from the ironmonger's in plastic drums. The handles would dig into my hands.

In the winter it was considered perfectly normal to have ice on the inside of our bedroom windows. I was often very cold in bed. My bed would be heaped high with thick, rough blankets and there would be coats placed on top of them for added warmth.

In the living room I would lie on the carpet in front of the gas fire to get warm while I watched *Jackanory* and *Blue Peter*. I had to light this fire with a match when I got home from school and I used to be scared anticipating the sudden 'boom' as it burst into life.

The telephone was in the hall and had a very short cable so it could not be moved anywhere else. Having a long conversation often meant wrapping up well in coats, hats and sometimes gloves. The draught would come through the front door as we sat on the bottom step of the stairs.

We had hot water bottles every night in the winter. These were lovely when they were warm but it was horrible to wake up with your feet on cold rubber. I can still picture my mum tipping the hot water bottle upside down and shaking it to test that the lid was on tightly before putting it under my covers.

The back porch was used to store perishable items such as milk before we had a fridge because it was very cold there.

Drying clothes was difficult. My dad built a huge clothes drying pulley out of wood which was hoisted up in the kitchen every day, loaded with garments. As the kitchen was small, this was suspended over the kitchen table. We got used to being dripped on as we ate.

Just after my sixth birthday, Harold Wilson introduced the British Standard Time experiment. The clocks were jiggled about with so that we had to walk to school in the dark. We were issued with reflective arm bands to wear over our duffle coats to stop us being run over. This lasted until I was nine.

There was something quite exciting about going to school under the cloak of darkness. The light from the lampposts made our arm bands glow bright yellow. As you walked along all you could see, far into the distance was a string of yellow rectangles bobbing up and down in the blackness.

# 6 ~ Colour TV

As far as I can remember we always had a television, although we didn't get a colour one until 1977 when I was fourteen. There really weren't a lot of programmes to choose from as there were only three channels and transmission ended at about midnight. I certainly didn't watch a lot of TV as a child but at about one-thirty each lunchtime our black and white set was switched on so I could see *Watch with Mother*. This was a collection of different programmes aimed at preschoolers consisting of stories acted out by puppets, cartoons and in one case live rodents!

I used to get very excited when it was getting close to the time of broadcasting. It was undoubtedly the highlight of my day. The ironic thing was, I didn't ever watch it with my mother. She used to go into the kitchen with her radio on and shut the door!

I would sit completely transfixed as a Dalmatian dog puppet ambled its way clumsily and painstakingly across the screen. It was the most basic, unrealistic puppet you could imagine. Maybe the creators thought simplicity was the way to go. I adored dogs and would fantasise about having my own spotty dog one day as I watched. I did actually get a Dalmatian when I was thirty-three so maybe those early influences ran really deep.

We had a TV repair man who would come in a van, take the set away during one of its frequent breakdowns and bring it back, renewed a few days later. Depression ensued as we stared at the empty space in the corner. My parents said these repairs cost a fortune so it was always a bit tense when something did go wrong.

The first time I ever saw a colour television set was on the 14th of November 1973, when I had just turned eleven. I know the date because it was the day Princess Anne married Mark Phillips. All the mums were looking forward to this event being on TV. One of my mum's friends (whom I called Auntie) was quite well off and had bought a colour television especially for the occasion.

My whole family dressed up and trundled off on the bus to this lady's house, joining dozens of her friends and neighbours, all there for the privilege of watching the royal wedding in glorious colour. My auntie had paid £350 for the set. This might not sound a lot now but the average weekly wage for a man in 1973 was only just over £40. It would be the equivalent of spending £4,240 on a TV today.

We all gathered around the huge TV, adults on sofas, chairs and stools and us kids on the floor. The set was ceremoniously switched on. Sausage rolls and pineapple and cheese cubes on sticks were passed around. It was one of those TVs with an enormous, fat back and was incredibly heavy. Auntie solemnly drew apart the concertinaed, sliding wooden shutters and the treat began.

There was a collective 'ooh!' as the picture appeared. The colours were what I can only describe as 'very vivid.' Everyone looked like they were wearing shocking pink lipstick and skin tones were mostly orange. There seemed to be a lot of lime green on the screen as well.

At the age of eleven, and being a real tomboy, I was keen to see this new colour TV but not the least bit interested in a royal wedding. The other kids and I began to fidget and mess around and we were soon put out of the viewing room to play elsewhere.

At school they had a TV for important events, although I can't recall at this distance what these events actually were. It was on a high stand with wheels underneath and would be wheeled into the assembly hall to great excitement.

Probably the most exciting event I watched on our black and white set was when Neil Armstrong first set foot on the moon when I was six. It was the first all night broadcast and that famous small step for a man happened just before 4am, British time. I'm grateful that my parents realised what a historic moment it was and got us out of bed to watch it in our pyjamas.

I remember sleepily kneeling on my sister's bed to look at the moon from her window immediately after this and feeling a bit confused that I couldn't see Neil and Buzz walking around up there.

## 7 ~ MONEY

They played a very mean trick on me when I was eight. On February 15th, 1971 the monetary system that I had just painstakingly mastered was abolished and 'new money' came in.

Now, to anyone who is not old enough to remember 'old money', let me tell you quite frankly that it was insane. Called L.S.D (very appropriately) there were 12 pennies in a shilling and 240 pennies (or 20 shillings) in a pound. Confused yet? You will be!

Half of a penny was called a ha'penny, 3p was a thick, brass 12 sided coin called a thrup'ny bit and sixpence was a thin, silver coin called a tanner. A shilling was called a bob. Two shillings was a florin, and two & six (shillings) was called a half crown. Ten bob was a pink bank note and a guinea was slightly more than a pound (21 shillings).

Can you imagine having just mastered all that and then someone telling you to forget about it all and think 'new money?'

One new penny was worth 2.4 old pennies but rapid inflation meant that 1 new pence soon bought less than the old. The old shilling was now worth 5 new pence. The funny thing about decimalisation is that we kids grasped it a lot easier than the adults, and we quickly took advantage of this by trying to fool the local shopkeepers into giving us more sweets than the money we had warranted.

We had also just learned to measure things in feet and inches, weigh things in pounds and ounces and how to tell the difference between a pint, a quart and a gallon. All this had to be unlearned later as we went metric.

There was never a lot of money to go around in our house, in spite of both parents working. I had quite a few part-time jobs. My first was a paper round when I was scarcely tall enough to reach the letter boxes. Some of the flats I had to go into seemed creepy in the dark mornings, with their communal landings and heavy fire doors that swung shut behind you. The bag of papers was very heavy and many a time my Chopper bike and I went sideways and hit the deck and all the papers spilled out onto the wet pavement. I got paid £1.89 for my first week's work.

When I was fifteen, I worked for two weeks in the summer in a general grocer's shop. I got £15 for each week. I bought a pair of Lee Cooper denim dungarees, a stripey, fluffy jumper and some shoes with my wages.

At seventeen, I got a good job, working in the wine and cigarettes section of a large supermarket. I enjoyed this job. I worked with two tall, blond lads who towered above me. The employers had somehow failed to realise I was underage to sell alcohol. The only problem with this job was that they gave me an overall that was about six sizes too big and almost trailed on the floor. I would reach up to get a bottle from the top shelf and the hem of my overall would hook over one of the bottles on the bottom shelf. When I walked away, I'd drag it with me and it would smash on the floor. Oops!

When I was about thirteen, my sister left school and got quite an unusual job. It was around 1975 and of course mobile phones were way in the future. The company my sister got the job with provided pagers to businessmen. As they drove around in their cars they could still receive messages from people who wanted to contact them. The caller would leave a message by landline with my sister and then she would page the clients and relay the messages.

She was paid monthly, so had a long wait for her first wages. Eventually the big day came and as we sat on the settee in our living room she ceremoniously opened the small manila envelope and spread nine crisp ten pound notes across the seat between us.

We had seldom seen so much money in cash in the one place. We spent ages talking of all the things she could buy but we both knew she would spend it all on clothes. I was allowed to choose one present to be bought with a little of the money and after a lot of thought I decided on a Beach Boys LP.

# 8 ~ SUNDAY SCHOOL

When my parents got married back in 1952, there was a bit of a hoo-hah because they were of different religions. After my sister and I came along, they felt it was important to send us to Sunday school from a very young age. They didn't argue over whose church we should attend. They simply sent us to the nearest one which happened to be a Methodist church. (Neither of them were Methodists.)

I don't know what this church was like for an adult in the mid sixties, but for a kid going to Sunday school there it was mostly great fun.

Once a month we had to attend real church services which were a lot harder, because they were so formal. We were both wrigglers and gigglers when very young, so it was hard to keep still and silent during the solemn ceremonies.

There was a lady organist who was both very tall and blind. For some reason we were frightened of her. My sister used to try to scare me by telling me she was walking up behind me, and then she would fall about laughing when I looked around in fright.

The best part about Sunday school though, was the singing. We sang many modern, groovy hymns which were mainly up-tempo. These songs were often composed especially for children and had 'actions' or hand, arm and leg movements to go along with the singing. It was basically like being in Take That, before they got too old to do the 'Pray' dance.

There we would stand, singing our little hearts out, flinging our arms wide, climbing imaginary steps, even rocking the imaginary baby Jesus in our arms. There was a lot of swaying and clapping too. It was brilliant fun!

During the monthly church service a huge wooden plate was passed along from seat to seat for the collection. Were each given a chunky, brass thrupenny bit to drop in as our contribution. We dreaded taking the plate and passing it along in case we dropped it, which actually happened to one unfortunate child one Sunday. The noise was deafening as the substantial pile of coins hit the floor and rolled all over the church.

One Sunday a horrible boy called Stephen chased my sister and I into the ladies' toilets threatening to give us a Chinese burn (painfully twisting your wrist.) We managed to get into a cubicle and locked the door. He began karate kicking the door.

My sister turned to me. 'Scream,' she urged. 'Scream as loud as you can!' I have no idea why she didn't just scream herself! So I let out a blood curdling sort of yodel and an adult came running in. After a brief explanation Stephen was carted off to face a telling-off.

My sister and I were left standing in the now silent toilet cubicle. Unfortunately, when I had screamed, the coin I had been clutching in my fist all morning slipped from my hand and fell into the toilet bowl. We stared down at my collection money, horrified at the thought of me being publicly shamed by having no money to put in the collection plate.

'You know what you are going to have to do, don't you?' said my heartless sister. I began to weep. The idea of the germs that might be in the toilet made me afraid I might end up dying of some unspecified disease.

'Come on, let me help you,' said my sister kindly. She undid my cuff and rolled up my sleeve. I looked at her with tears shining in my eyes.

'Just do it, quick!' she urged.

I plunged my hand into the toilet bowl, grabbed the thrupence and ran squealing to the sink where I desperately tried to work up a lather from the hard, dry block of pink carbolic soap.

As we walked back to the main part of the church I went to take my sister's hand as usual but she held it up away from me saying, 'better not. Don't want to catch the germs.'

## 9 ~ MILK

Where I live now, if you want milk you have to drive to the supermarket and get it. It comes in one litre cartons and will cost you about €1.18. When I was a child in the sixties of course, milk was always delivered by the milkman. The milk float would rattle slowly up the road, its electric engine whining and every few yards either the milkman himself or a lad employed to do most of the leg work would run up a path with a trio of glass pint bottles full of milk. The empties would be deftly swept up, deposited onto the back of the milk cart and on it would go. Late on Friday afternoons the milkman would call to every house on his milk round to collect payment.

Our milkman was called Joe. Joe was over six feet tall, quite thin and he always had an unlit pipe clamped between his teeth. He could still whistle with the pipe in place. All delivery men in those days seemed to whistle. He was a teddy boy with his hair fashioned into a quiff and elaborate lamb chop sideburns. He carried a short, stubby pencil behind his ear and wore black, woollen fingerless gloves. He kept the money in a leather satchel on his hip and carried a leather bound accounts book.

It was my job to pay Joe with the money left on the telephone stand in the hall. He would always hum a tuneless ditty while he totted up the money owed.

'Dah de-dah dah...That's three on Monday, four on Tuesday... De dah de...'

He would say 'Thanks, bab,' when I handed the coins over but he never once made eye contact.

You could buy bottles of orange juice from the milkman. Us kids would ask our mum for it but were always told it was too expensive. If you saw bottles of orange juice on someone's doorstep you knew they were quite well-to-do. There were two types of milk, which we referred to as 'Pas' and 'Stera.' These were abbreviations for pasteurised and sterilised. Pas came in a dumpy bottle with a foil top. Blue tits would often peck through the foil and sip from the inch of cream at the top of the bottle. Stera came in a tall thin bottle with a metal top like a beer bottle.

Most people had a strong preference for either Pas or Stera milk. If you were offered a cup of tea in someone's house you would generally have a quick glance at the table to see what kind of milk bottle was there before accepting.

Milk bottles being taken in off the sunny step early in the morning was a sign that all was well. If milk was left there for any length of time, someone would knock on the door to make sure the occupant of the house was alright.

At my infant school we were given a small bottle of milk each at the 11am breaktime. The milk monitor would hand out the milk and straws and for a few minutes we would all furiously sip together. We had a lot of wooden, outdoor classrooms which were called terrapins. The crate of milk would be left outside in the sun for two hours until needed, by which time it was less than palatable. So we didn't always look forward to milk time.

At home, when you had finished with a bottle of milk, you left the empty bottle on the doorstep. Most people would wash the bottle first, or at least rinse it. But careless types would just place the dirty bottles on the step ready for collection. My mum used the state of someone's empty milk bottles as a yardstick by which to judge whether they were a 'nice' family or not. Sometimes we would walk past a house and she would whisper, 'och, look at the state of their bottles!'

When I went to play with a new child after school I would be grilled when I got home as to what sort of family they were. The number one question was always, 'were their empties clean?' Of course, when you were a little kid, eagerly looking forward to a new game with a new friend, the last thing you would be doing as you entered their house was to check out the cleanliness of the milk bottles on their step. I quickly learned that the right answer was 'yes.' Then she was happy and so was I.

## 10 ~ SLEEP TO THE BEAT

I was born seven days after the Beatles released their first single, 'Love Me Do' so it seemed inevitable that their music would touch my young life in some way. It did, but in an indirect way.

Next door to us was a family with seven children. Big families were very common in those days. They ranged in age from my age up to about fifteen years older than me. Four of these lads were absolutely obsessed with the Beatles. To their great credit, each one had taught himself either guitar, bass or drums and they had very tuneful singing voices. For as long as I could remember, they had been a Beatles tribute band. They never played songs by anyone else. Only the Beatles. They took the name of their band from the name of the council estate we lived on, which was clever.

They had a shed which was part of the house and they used this as their rehearsal room. They painted the bare brick walls black and all their instruments and amplifiers were jammed in there. Most nights, especially in the summer they would practise in there with the door open while various young fans loitered in their garden, listening and smoking. All this activity occurred right under my bedroom window as the two houses were only feet apart.

Not only did these chaps sound just like the Beatles, they did their best to look exactly like them as well. The drummer did his best to look like Ringo, the lead guitarist was a dead ringer for George, and so on.

They wore a uniform of black jeans and black polo neck jumpers. They even dyed their hair black and had haircuts with long fringes. Their black hair contrasted strangely with their very pale skin.

On summer evenings we would be out on the Green, playing ball games or tig but at some point we would be called in and made to go to bed. It was always very hard to fall asleep when you could see that it was still light outside your bedroom curtains. In my case, however, I had the added distraction of a full volume pop band rehearsal going on a few feet away.

I would lie in my small bed, eyes open as the sounds of 'Ticket to Ride', 'She Loves You', and 'Love Me Do' rang out into the summer night. The lyrics would paint vivid stories in my head and I would eventually drift off to sleep to my own pop video.

The song I recall most clearly from those days went:

*Oh oh I... Never realised what a kiss could be...This could only happen to me... Can't you see... Can't you see?*

I was probably not all that familiar with the real Beatles. When I was six my mum was forty-two and my dad was fifty, so they were more keen on Jim Reeves, Miki and Griff, or Scottish music and weren't of an age to be Beatles fans. Nevertheless, every member of our family knew all the words to most of the Beatles songs thanks to the nightly concerts next door.

Sometimes I would be tempted to have a peek and I would tiptoe across to my window in my bare feet and peer out from behind the net curtain. The band would wave up at me and I would giggle and wave back.

I began playing the guitar myself when I was eight. Between the mock Beatles, my parents' records, my dad playing his guitar and both parents singing I had had a good grounding in the structure of song. Many nights of lying awake as my room filled with music taught me to love and understand melody and rhythm. As for the lyrics, they painted a picture of a world of romance that was yet far off. One where boys loved girls, girls left boys and boys cried.

Sometimes, during the day I was allowed into the actual rehearsal room. Me and the youngest child of their family would sneak in and gaze at the drum kit and amplifiers until an older boy would chase us out to play in their garden. A few of the lads rode motorbikes and there would generally be a bike parked in the shed in various states of repair along with the instruments. So the smell of gearbox oil always reminds me of the excitement of pop music. It was all totally glamorous to me, aged five or six. Not every kid had the Beatles living next door.

## 11 ~ THE TINY DRESS

When I was very little I used to love it when my mum cleared out our airing cupboard where the fresh laundry was kept, along with towels and blankets. When it was almost empty I would climb onto the wooden slatted shelves and make a den.

One day, I was playing in the airing cupboard when I found a tiny dress. It was in different shades of cerise and pink with vertical stripes. It reminded me of a stick of rock.

'Whose is this?' I asked my mum. She held it up and looked sad. 'It used to be yours,' she sighed. 'You were so little and sweet then.' Immediately I wanted to be the little, sweet girl who had worn the tiny dress. But I didn't know how.

I can still picture a lot of the outfits my sister and I wore. Often we were dressed the same. We had an old aunt who loved to knit us matching cardigans but they were always made of very itchy, rough wool and in dreadful colours. The worst of these was a cardigan in a sort of fisherman's rib stitch in a dirty, dark orange colour. My initial was embroidered on the pocket in green. We had to wear them whenever this aunt visited.

For Sunday school we were dressed up like toffs. We had matching crimplene dresses. Mine was lilac and my sister's was lemon. Along with these we wore white boaters with a very uncomfortable piece of elastic under the chin. We also had matching blazers; mine in red, hers in blue, with white trimmings. We wore these with white box pleat skirts.

We also had royal blue dresses with large white spots on, which flared out from the waist. It wasn't generally known that sunburn was dangerous in those days and one year when I was in the infant school, I got terrible sunburn. I can remember the feeling of that spotty dress on my poor over-tanned skin and when I see a photo of me in it, I can smell the Calamine lotion that was dabbed on as a cure.

I knew what clothes I felt comfortable in from a very early age. I always found girls' clothes uncomfortable and impractical. I'm allergic to lace and elasticated cuffs used to bring me out in wheals as well. I climbed a lot of trees and played a lot of football so dresses were out as I grew older and could choose what I wanted to wear.

Very occasionally there would be a special event and my mother would try to force me into a dress. One such occasion was my ninth birthday party. We had some relatives staying and they told my mum that if I were their daughter they would make sure I wore a dress for my party. My mum felt under pressure to force me to conform so I was given an ultimatum: wear the dress or miss my own party. I still remember the dress; it was sky blue with a lot of sequins on it. I had no difficulty in deciding and indeed spent my own party shut in my bedroom in disgrace.

One of the most way-out fashion creations of my childhood was hot pants. Hot pants were shorts with a bib and braces attached. The braces crossed over at the back. My mum had a friend who was a keen knitter. She used to make quite cool outfits for my Action Man.

There was a fête coming up at my junior school. We heard there was going to be a children's hot pants competition. It sounds a bit dubious now but back then it was completely normal. My mum asked her friend if she could come up with anything. She said she'd see what she could do.

A while later she turned up at our doorstep carefully carrying two brown paper parcels. One for me and one for my sister. Inside were lime green, knitted hot pants. I think we had our doubts about them as we paraded around the ring with all the other hot pants wearers.

We didn't win anything. Fortunately there are no photographs.

## 12 ~ BUTLINS

The picture of me on the front of this book was taken during my first ever holiday, to Butlins Clacton in the summer of 1966, when I was three years old. The original photograph it is taken from is an 8.5 x 6.5 inch picture taken by a Butlins photographer. There are three other children in the larger photo. The boy in it is wearing a bow tie. I am wearing my red plastic leather-look jacket and a toy watch.

I actually remember having the photo taken as indeed I remember a lot of that holiday. I had been left by my parents at a children's puppet show and that is why I look so worried! I was wondering if they were ever coming back.

We must have travelled there by coach. My first memory of the holiday is arriving at the chalet and being very excited that we were somewhere different.

There was a children's playground with one of those things that looked a bit like a see-saw but which rocked from end to end. My sister and I were on this ride when an American little girl came up and asked if she could play with us. She was staying in a chalet near ours and we became firm friends for the rest of our stay there. The three of us were in floods of tears when we had to say goodbye.

The little girl's name was Jodie. When I was older, I used to imagine that it might have been the actress Jodie Foster, although in reality I don't quite think she'd have really been at Butlins in Clacton in 1966.

I still have a badge from there. It's a cloth badge with 'Butlins Beaver Club' embroidered on it.

A vivid memory is my first donkey ride which took place on the beach with my dad walking beside me, along with the owner of the donkeys. I remember the creak of the saddle and even the donkey's name. He was called Nobby. Of course there were a lot of tears when I realised I couldn't take him home with me, as I had fallen in love with him.

There was a swimming pool there with glass walls and it was fascinating to see people swimming underwater. I have a feeling the glass wall formed part of the dining room, although I can't be sure half a century later. I was considered too young for swimming but my sister who was six went to a children's 'Learn to Swim' class. She was so traumatised by what happened that she never learned to swim in later life, claiming that the instructor tied a rope around her waist and threw her in!

She also took part in a little girl's beauty contest and was very sad not to win anything. She still has the photo of them standing in a line each holding a placard with a number on it.

In the summer of 1974 we went to Butlins again. This time we went to the Pwllheli in Wales. My sister's friend came with us. They were 14 and I was 11. We were all three at the sulky 'I'm so bored' age. It rained continuously for the whole fortnight and was freezing cold. We spent most of time going to and fro on a cable car, or roller-skating to the sound of 'Kung Fu Fighting' by Carl Douglas.

My sister's friend and I went swimming in the sea in the rain with the result that I developed one of my very frequent bouts of tonsillitis. I had made a friend there who was a boy called Brian. It was a kind of innocent pre-teen first holiday romance. I lay on the sofa in the chalet with my throat throbbing in pain while he loyally sat chatting to me as the rain beat against the window. The camp doctor said it was the worst case of tonsillitis he had ever seen.

The three of us girls didn't want to return home looking pale so we bought some fake tanning cream. We all put it on one night but nothing much happened and we thought it was a very ineffectual product. We kept putting more and more on but we didn't get any closer to that holiday glow.

When we woke up in the morning and saw each other's faces we were horrified. We were all three dark orange. That's my lasting memory of that holiday. A throat that felt full of barbed wire, the torrential rain and my orange face and palms.

## 13 ~ PARCELS

Every year at Christmas there were two parcels we really looked forward to receiving. The first of these was my dad's Works Christmas Box. He worked in a factory and every year the workers received a Christmas parcel each, containing all manner of seasonal foods. This was probably the forerunner to the annual Christmas cash bonus.

It's really quite hard now to imagine a couple of kids getting excited about a box of groceries but we anticipated it as eagerly as if it were a box of toys.

The items the box contained were typically a Christmas pudding, a packet of custard, nuts, a box of biscuits, a tin of pears, a packet of jelly and things of that nature. It was delivered by someone who had a car because my dad travelled the two miles to and from work by bicycle. The large cardboard box generally had a Christmas bow on the top and a bit of Christmas paper lining the inside.

The entire family would gather around the box and my dad would open it as we pushed our eager little faces closer to examine the packets of food.

'Ooh Dad! Strawberry Angel Delight!'

'Look Mum! Party Rings!'

We ate very plain food during the rest of the year so tasty fancy puddings and biscuits were really something to get excited about.

The funny thing was, every year the box got smaller and smaller. It wasn't just us getting bigger. It was the cost of living or cutbacks or maybe a general decline in the generosity of the employers. My dad took voluntary redundancy when I was about eighteen, as he was then 62 and not in great health. When I was a very small child there would be about 40 items in the Christmas Box. In his last one there was a small Christmas pudding in a red plastic bowl, a packet of custard creams, some nuts and a Christmas card without his name on it, printed with *Best Wishes* at the bottom and the name of the factory.

The other parcel came by post van. It was generally the size of a couple of suitcases and contained presents for all the family from our auntie in California. My mum got tea towels, tights, gloves, headscarves and slippers. Dad always received shirts. These used to make us shriek in amazement as they were the most gaudy shirts imaginable. I remember one being yellow, purple and pink in alternate wide vertical stripes. They were very jazzy for my conservative father and he never wore any of them. They were also always far too big. He was barely five feet tall and weighed less than ten stone. We didn't know what to do with them so they hung in his wardrobe for years, untouched.

There were clothes for my sister and I but mostly there were toys. One year we had a kaleidoscope each. These were fat tubes that you looked down. As you twisted the disc at the end, coloured beads fell into mirrored segments making vivid patterns. I just can't imagine modern kids getting excited about these either. But we were delighted with them. We used to walk in slow motion to each other's rooms, carefully cradling the kaleidoscope to show off a particularly pretty pattern without jolting the beads out of place. Another year we got bagatelles which were mini pinball machines.

One year we received a big doll each. I was never interested in dolls but this one was rather special and sort of fascinated me. My sister's doll had a ginger, bobbed hairstyle and a pull chord in its back.

'My eyes are blue 'cause I eat carrots' it exclaimed over and over again in a strong American accent. She was forbidden to take it to school but did so anyway, unable to resist showing it off. A big boy broke it and from then on it was cute but mute.

My doll was very unusual. It was large and solid and wore a pink romper suit with a rigid hood trimmed with fur. Now try to imagine this if you can. The head had three faces. One face showed at a time peeking out of the hood while the other two were inside the hood. A lever under its collar at the back selected which face was at the front. If you are thinking this sounds sinister looking you are completely right. It was scary!

I tried to love it and called it Belinda. One face was laughing, one was crying and one was sleeping. As if that wasn't eerie enough, the doll made appropriate noises for each face. I wasn't sorry the day she stopped gurgling/ sobbing/ snoring and froze with her eyes closed for good. Into the airing cupboard she went and I went back to Action Man.

## 14 ~ BATH TIME

I love getting together with friends of my own age and reminiscing about our sixties and seventies childhoods. But if there's one thing we all agree on it is this. Children in those days weren't very clean!

It was completely normal to have a bath and hair wash only once a week. Nobody seemed to have showers in their houses. It cost extra money to heat enough water for a bath and this was regarded as precious. Multiple people would use the same bath water. Usually the kids would be bathed first. Siblings were bathed together.

When we were very little our mum would supervise the whole bath. For a treat each child would be swished from one end of the bath to the other while our mum sang this song. The first part was traditional but the second part, we had added as a cheeky reference to our dad. It went like this:

*Shoogie shaggy over the glen. Mummy's pet and Daddy's hen*
*Daddy always gets in a mood when he has to do the curtains.*

Our dad could be grumpy when he had to carry out annoying DIY tasks such as the one where he had to stand on a table and insert curtain hooks into the newly laundered curtains. Getting the spacing right often required undoing it and starting from scratch again.

Our bath was in a tiny room with just a wash-hand basin next to it. The toilet was in a separate room. Aunties would buy us bath salts for Christmas presents. They were square heavy tablets that you dropped into the water. They would slowly dissolve making the water smell nice but leaving uncomfortable, gritty crumbs on the bottom of the bath. We also used bath crystals which were usually purple. My sister used to persuade me to put a bath crystal up each nostril and would then have a good laugh as my eyes watered with the stinging sensation.

As young kids, my sister and I were always fighting. Bath time was an activity guaranteed to produce spats as we were stuck in the same bath together. As we got older my mum would go downstairs and leave us to bathe ourselves. This often resulted in mayhem as we whacked each other with wet cloths and generally squabbled and fought until one of us started crying. Mum would come thundering up the stairs in a temper. Her feet thudding on each step inducing more and more panic. Then we would be soundly slapped.

The bathroom was completely unheated so bath time could be unpleasant in the winter. One day, my parents saw an advertisement in the newspaper for a combined light/heater. It was quite a large contraption which screwed into the light fitting directly over the bath. On its inaugural session heating the room, my sister and I sat underneath it feeling nice and cosy and soon got down to the important business of whacking each other with wet flannels.

In an instant the whole contraption exploded. This was probably caused by a splash of water landing on the hot surface. We were sprayed with red hot bits of glass and sharp shards of thin metal. We both leaped out of the bath, unfortunately jumping onto more sharp pieces of the device, cutting our feet too. We ran completely naked, screaming down the stairs. The sight of each other streaming with blood from various cuts made us cry even harder. Amazingly neither of us were seriously hurt but we were very shaken.

If that had happened nowadays the company would have been sued as a matter of course. As it was, my mum did write to them and complain. I seem to remember they wrote a stuffy letter back saying it had been our own fault and that was the end of the matter.

After our bath we would sit wrapped in towels by the gas fire eating a supper which was usually cheese on toast. *Steptoe and Son* would be on the television. Then we would go to bed.

# 15 ~ COMICS

Comics were a big part of life during my childhood. Some of them were delivered through the door with the daily newspaper and others I bought from the newsagent. I don't remember ever getting the toddler comics like *Twinkle*. I jumped straight to *The Beano*, which was a fabulous comic. My favourite character from *The Beano* was Dennis the Menace and his naughty, wild coated dog Gnasher. I had no idea the 'G' was meant to be silent in Gnasher's name so to this day I think of him as Guh-nasher!

A very rare treat was getting *The Beano Annual*, which was a large hardback book full of stories about your favourite characters. I had one which had a drawing of a Dennis and Gnasher's treehouse on the back cover. I adored this. It was complete with a biscuit bone dispensing machine for Gnasher and a lemonade dispenser for Dennis. It had paw-print wallpaper on the wall and a secret emergency escape hatch. I wished I could have a treehouse just like it.

I wasn't so keen on *The Dandy*. Desperate Dan was a popular character but I didn't like his face. A comic I loved was the double edition, *Whizzer and Chips*. You got two comics in one. *Chips* was the best.

My sister got *Jackie* magazine, aimed at slightly older girls. It seemed sophisticated and had pin-ups inside. She had Marc Bolan on her wall. I had Michael Jackson, David Cassidy and later, the Bay City Rollers. I used to trade things with her to get the posters she didn't want.

Some giant posters came in three parts. You'd get legs the first week, a torso the second and finally the head. These were carefully fitted together after the long wait for all the pieces and pinned to the wall.

During arguments, a popular tactic was to threaten to rip each other's posters. We rarely ever actually carried out these threats though.

I used to get a magazine called *Mates* which favoured the Bay City Rollers and had a lot of free gifts such as a tartan cardboard photo frame. There was also a magazine called *Supersonic* which once had a free gold coloured Bay City Rollers seven inch flexi single record. It was Mike Mansfield interviewing the Rollers. Mine had a kink in it and so you could just hear him saying 'hiya lads!' over and over again as the needle of my record player hopped repeatedly back to the same spot.

The best part about *Jackie* was the famous problem page, Cathy and Claire. Girls would write in, usually about problems regarding boys they had crushes on who weren't that interested in them.

*I love him so much, but he hasn't even noticed me.*

Cathy and Claire would write back with very sensible advice.

I once wrote a thirty-two page letter to Cathy and Claire. I composed it in my bedroom with my bookcase against the door barring nosy intruders, pouring out all my troubles. I can't remember exactly what was in it but I'd hazard a guess it was to do with being shy and not having many friends. Oh, and of course that my parents didn't understand me. I was about fifteen then and going through a very unhappy phase.

It felt good to get it all off my chest but after I had addressed the envelope I began to have serious doubts. What if the ladies in the local post office saw it when it was taken from the letter box and saw who it was addressed to? Might they get curious and open it? If they did, all my secrets would be known to the world. What if Cathy and Claire thought I was a complete freak? What if they contacted my parents?

On reflection it was just too risky to actually send it. Of course, now I had the problem of how to get rid of the thing. I couldn't just shove it in the bin where my parents might find it.

In the end I waited until I was alone in the house and took it down the bottom of the garden and placed it in my dad's brazier. There I burned it, carefully poking the pieces around with a stick until they were just black, flaky shreds.

## 16 ~ REELY FUNNY

Around 1969 my dad bought a massive Grundig reel to reel tape recorder. It weighed a ton and would get red hot when it was switched on for any length of time. This was before cassette tapes. The tapes were open reel; each one the size of a large saucer. The tape was started and stopped by a very heavy lever. It cost forty-four pounds which was a small fortune back then.

My dad was one of eight and my mum one of four so we had plenty of aunts and uncles who were flung as far afield as Australia, New Zealand and America. My dad liked to send them tape recordings of us kids singing, playing our recorders and later, me playing my guitar. Sometimes we recorded songs where the whole family sang.

These recording sessions were excruciating for me and my sister for one reason. We simply could not stop laughing when we were supposed to perform.

My dad would become very nervous by the whole recording occasion and the switching of the lever to 'Record.' He so badly wanted everything to go smoothly and we could hear the tension in his voice as he counted us in. He only had to say 'go' and we would absolutely fall about in uncontrollable fits of laughter. You could call it performance anxiety. Or you could just say that we were two daft sisters who lost control of ourselves when we were attempting to do anything together which required us to be serious. My dad would get progressively angrier towards us with each take and the pressure just got worse and worse. The relatives seemed to enjoy the finished results however, so this was something we were required to do quite frequently.

As we got a bit older, us kids used the tape recorder to record *Top of the Pops* from the television and *The Top Forty* countdown from the radio.

When I was ten I used to walk home from junior school at lunchtime and eat my lunch in comfort watching *Crown Court*. My sister was about thirteen then and had a best friend called Jane. They would both come to our house from the 'Big School' around the same time to eat their lunch. One day they came home giggling about a plan they had hatched to get revenge on a teenage boyfriend who had dumped Jane for another girl. They asked me to comply.

There was show on local radio at the time where people rang the station and after chatting to the DJ, listed items they wanted to buy or sell over the air. The plan was that Jane, egged on by my sister, would phone in advertising a few imaginary items for sale and give her ex-boyfriend's number. He would then be pestered all day by folk phoning his house asking to buy things. She was incredibly convincing as a housewife wanting to make some pin money by selling a tartan skirt, a riding hat, and two pairs of wellies; a red pair and a blue pair.

My job was twofold. First I had to tape the whole performance from the radio onto the tape recorder. We played it back over and over, laughing our socks off. We then took it in turns to ring the ex-boyfriend's house using various accents and voices asking for wellies, skirts or hats.

I don't think any of us made it back to school that afternoon. We were too busy quoting the poor lad's mum shouting, 'for the last time, there are no bloody wellies here. Okay?!!!' Then we'd laugh until our sides ached.

Looking back, we laughed a lot in those long gone days. I think if I saw an antique reel to reel tape recorder now it would set me off giggling even to this day.

## 17 ~ MY UNIQUE SKATEBOARD

My dad had been a carpenter when he was younger so I often received home made toys. One of these was a beautiful white rocking horse with a red mane and black hooves and tail. It was my favourite toy for a long time. One day, when admittedly I was too big for it and no longer using it, my parents told me they were going to give it to their friend's little boy who was younger. I was quite upset about losing it, because I was proud that Dad had made it for me.

At the age of ten there was a great craze for walking around on stilts. My dad quickly made me a pair. The handles were planed round and smooth. I soon got the hang of stilt walking and could run up and down the garden, steps and all quite easily. He then added blocks to the foot pieces to make them higher so it became more of a challenge.

My sister and I live in different countries now but she told me not long ago that when she pictures me, she always thinks of a skinny ten year old flying about on wooden stilts!

Space hoppers were very popular. This was a giant orange balloon that you sat on, holding onto to two little handles. You bounced along using your feet to launch yourself. I never had one but I had a go on one and discovered it took a lot of energy.

What I really wanted was a pogo stick. I asked for one over and over but was told we couldn't afford it. I decided to take matters into my own hands. I found a couple of old bed springs and nailed these to a small plank of wood. I didn't know how to attach the upright pole so instead, I nailed a pair of old shoes to the other side of the plank. I put my feet in the shoes and tried to launch myself but all that happened was that I fell over.

Dad made me a sledge once. We had a lot of snow one winter and all my friends bought lightweight plastic sledges. Mine was made of sturdy wood and in the design of a traditional Father Christmas sleigh. Unfortunately it weighed more than me and was very hard to tow uphill. Even when facing down a slope it would just sit there rather than speed down the hill so I always had to coax it down the slope.

I think I was about 14 when skateboards became a craze where I lived, which would make it about 1976 or 1977. It seemed to take off overnight and suddenly everyone was doing it. The skateboard itself was expensive as was the safety equipment.

My dad very kindly made me one in his garden shed. He cleverly carved it out of one piece of wood so it had a kick tail and all the right contours. He put wheels from my old roller skates on it and painted it light green. I made my own knee and elbow pads out of football socks, sponge and elastic but had no helmet. This ensemble enabled me to join in the skateboarding fun and the only disadvantage was that I could only travel in straight lines as the wheels were fixed. I never got a real one but I remember my skateboard fondly and the kindness of my dad in making it for me.

## 18 ~ BIKES

My first bike wasn't just a Christmas present. I used it to test Father Christmas because my friend Wendy kept telling me he didn't exist. I asked for a blue bike in the normal way with a letter to Santa. But on Christmas Eve, after I had gone to bed, I opened my bedroom window and shouted, 'please can my bike have a bell and a boot!' When I came down at the crack of dawn on Christmas morning, there it sat, complete with bell and a large boot at the back. Proof! Put THAT in your pipe and smoke it, Wendy!

It was a large three wheeler and I promptly set about filling the boot with all my teddies and took them for a ride around the block. My sister had a pair of fairy princess sparkly 'glass' (Perspex) slippers that year among other things. They had a small stiletto type of heel. They were pink with glitter embedded in them. She climbed onto my bike for a go, still wearing these shoes and as she began to pedal, both heels snapped off. There were a few tears that Christmas.

My first go on a two wheeler was during parents' evening at my infant school. While my mum was inside talking to my teachers, I waited in the playground along with a few other kids. One had a two wheeler with small, thick, white tyres and he let me have a go. The boy whose bike it was shouted encouragement for me to put both feet on the pedals and there it was. I was suddenly balancing on a two wheeler by myself. What a strange sensation it was.

I had my sister's hand-me-down bike later which had seen better days. I cycled to school every day and it served me well. But what I really wanted was either a Raleigh Chopper or a Mobo Cross 2000. Both had long, fancy saddles so you could give your friends 'backies' in style. Not to mention the high rise handlebars, a stand and a gear stick. I saved up every penny I could from pocket money and my paper round. It was going to take a long time as the Chopper cost £33.

Then one magical Christmas morning, I came down and it was waiting for me in the living room. Sleek, shiny and very purple. I adored that bike. I could never quite believe it was mine.

The novelty never wore off. For the whole time I owned it, until I was sixteen, I was very proud of my Chopper. Amazingly, it was never stolen. I say that because I had a habit of cycling to the shops, leaving my bike outside and then after buying what I wanted, I would walk home without a backward glance, forgetting I had cycled there.

'Oh Golly!' I'd run all the way back to the shops and it would always be waiting outside the shop, just where I had left it.

I had a best friend when I was about eleven called Gillian and she had an identical bike. We really thought we were something as we rode around together. I would go on many errands for my mum. She had a friend who lived two miles away and I was forever delivering or collecting things from her house by bicycle.

There was one aspect of riding my Chopper which still makes me go pink to this day and that was that I had the concept of gears back to front. The bike had three gears, operated by a stick shift on the crossbar. For some reason, I thought that you were supposed to start in third gear, shift to second as you built up speed and finally cruise along at high speed in first gear. I believed this right up until I learned to drive. When the instructor told me to start off in first gear I exclaimed, 'oh! It's the opposite of a bike then?'

Only then did it dawn on me why I had struggled so much. It was so hard to get going, pushing the stiff pedals around and my little legs had been a blur as I tried to keep up with them whizzing around as I sped along in first gear.

## 19 ~ CONQUERING LONELINESS

Children played out in the street a lot when I was young. There would be crazes for certain games and suddenly everyone in the street was doing the same thing.

Skipping was often in fashion. You could skip on your own of course but we liked to have a person at each end, turning the rope while the skipper chanted rhymes and performed actions:

*Not last night, but the night before. 24 Robbers came knocking at my door.*
*I went out to let them in and this is what they said to me.*
*Spanish lady, turn right round. Spanish lady, touch the ground.*
*Spanish lady do some kicks. Spanish lady, do the splits!*

If you didn't have two rope turners, you would tie one end to a lamppost which worked just as well.

Queenie was a game involving throwing a ball with your back turned and guessing who had caught it and hidden it:

*Queenie, Queenie, who's got the ball? Is he fat or is he tall? Is he like a rolling ball?*

'The farmer's in his den' was another chanting game for small children. People were alternately selected to represent the farmer, his wife, the child, the dog and the bone while the other children danced in a ring, holding hands, around them. We could barely contain our excitement as the end of the game approached. The last verse of the song and dance involved everybody converging on the last person chosen and patting them repeatedly on the head (a little too hard) while singing:

*We all pat the bone. We all pat the bone. Ee aye addy oh, we all pat the bone!*

In autumn, the game of conkers was very popular. For the benefit of anyone not familiar with this, a conker is the fruit inside a horse chestnut seed. We would crack open the prickly casing and collect the shiny brown conkers to take home. A shoe lace was threaded through the conker and tied in a knot underneath. We would do all sorts of things to strengthen the conker before doing battle. Soaking it in vinegar was one method and baking it in the oven was another.

To play conkers, the first person holds their conker out at arms length, suspended by the lace, like a pendulum. The other person tries to hit this with their own conker using a swiping motion. The loser is the one whose conker disintegrates first. The winning conker is known by how many battles it has won. Thus a sixer had smashed six other conkers in battle. Conkers were swapped and admired and even bought and sold.

One October I had carefully collected my conkers, baked them, soaked them and fitted them with laces. I was probably about nine. Unfortunately, I was going through a 'no friends' phase that children go through from time to time. I was very sad that I had no one to have a contest with.

My dad called me into the kitchen.

'I've found you a new pal to play conkers with. He's in the glory hole.' he grinned. The glory hole was a tiny cupboard under the stairs with a sloping roof. I was very short for my age so I could easily stand up in there.

Intrigued, I opened the door. He had wedged a walking stick between the two walls of the cupboard. From this he had suspended one of my conkers on its lace. It hung there inviting me to take a shot. I was delighted and it kept me entertained all evening.

Yes, I know what you are thinking. Why didn't my dad just play a game of conkers with me himself? I don't really know the answer to that. It had something to do with there being a clear cut line between parents and children, at least in my family. They didn't really play games with us. But at the time he cared enough to help. And that made all the difference to me, at nine years of age.

## 20 ~ GAMES AND TOYS

Moving Stairs was a game my sister and I made up and loved to play. One of us would lie on our back with our knees bent together in front of us and our feet flat on the floor. We would extend our arms as railings. The other one would stand on the knees of the person who was being the moving stair, holding hands. Then the person on the bottom would rotate their knees, trying to make the other one fall off. You generally got a foot in the stomach, or sometimes the face when the person fell, but for some reason the game used to really make us laugh.

Most of the time though, I played alone. My sister seemed to have lots of friends and was always out playing with them. I had only two preschool friends, both boys; both a year older than me. They were the sons of two of Mum's friends. I didn't see them that often.

When I played alone I would sit behind the sofa. It was quite close to the wall so I was almost in a little tent. My two favourite games were farm animals and Lego. I also liked to play with small cowboy and Indian figures and I had soldiers and a fort.

I loved to play with my Action Man. I had the Action Man with the blond painted on hair. For birthdays and Christmas I would get accessories. A fun one was a horse which I think was meant for the Lone Ranger or Tonto, but Action Man fitted onto it. It was beige and had a white mane and you could take the saddle and bridle on and off. I also had a diving set for him.

Another bit of Action Man gear I enjoyed was a whole polar expedition set. There was a sledge, three different coloured huskies and all the harnesses, plus a big, orange tent. Action Man himself had all the snow gear, a red parka with a furry hood, ski poles, skis, goggles and snowshoes. It snowed the Christmas I got this as a present. My well meaning father erected the tent for me and nailed it onto a piece of hardboard. I was secretly very disappointed as it meant I could no longer take the tent up and down but all in all it was a fantastic present

I was able to play with this lovely toy in real snow. I gave my mum the honour of naming the three huskies which I harnessed and unharnessed all day long and she said, 'call them Whiskey, Brandy and Sherry.' I wanted her to feel involved so pretended to use these names but really I didn't like the names and when I was by myself they were called different names, the lead dog always being called Bruce.

I had another action figure called Tommy Gunn. I remember other people had the Action Man with gripping hands, eagle eyes and real hair. My sister had Sindy and Barbie but could never resist trying to restyle their hair, which always went wrong, so they were practically bald.

I never had any Airfix sets but I did once have a mini Mechano set. I made a working guillotine (a charming toy for a little girl) but I hadn't grasped the concept that all the bolts had to be tight so it was kind of wobbly.

Every Christmas there was a toy everybody else seemed to have that you wanted and never got. For me that toy was a game called Raving Bonkers. It was two robots in a boxing ring and when one landed a successful blow the other one's head shot up! It looked brilliant on the TV Advert. I seem to remember it was £6.99.

I always wanted a toy called an Etch-A-Sketch but never got one. I can clearly remember asking a boy home to tea, purely because he had an Etch-A-Sketch which I wanted to have ago on. It was a case of, 'come to tea. Oh, and don't forget your Etch-A-Sketch!'

## 21 ~ PLAYING HOUSE

Like a lot of mums of that era, my mum was an agent for a popular catalogue selling clothes, toys and household goods. My sister and I loved it when she got a new catalogue. We would immediately make lists of all the fabulous new toys we wanted for Christmas, even if it was months away.

We used her spare order forms to make up imaginary orders costing hundreds of pounds. But the most fun we got from the catalogues came from last season's book.

Cut out doll books were very popular in the sixties. The doll was printed on the cardboard back of the book. You cut it out and stood it up and then cut out all the clothing printed on the inner pages, pinning them on the doll with paper tabs.

We had a variation of this game. We would get last season's catalogue and choose a woman and a man from the fashion models to be the parents of our family. These were carefully selected for looks and style. We would cut them out and then choose and cut out children, pets and a whole house full of furniture and leisure equipment. We would prop the furniture up against the skirting boards in our bedrooms and then visit each other's paper houses, commenting on the items selected and making up conversations between the paper characters. We were really practising for the day when we'd have a home of our own. We were finding out our tastes in sofas, curtains and clothing.

My sister was quite sophisticated at this game. I tended to want to cut out all the pets in the pet bed section and think up names for them and I also spent a long time choosing the bikes for my family. I wasn't so interested in what colour my kitchen blinds should be.

Occasionally we would both select the same outstanding item and argue over it, which often ended up in a tug of war, where the coveted paper possession would get ripped and have to be Sellotaped together when we had found a compromise and made friends.

We also had a little house under the apple tree at the very end of our large garden. There were no walls but we used the apple tree to support wooden shelves. My dad got hold of a huge pile of linoleum tiles one day. They were all different colours and we spread them on the earthen floor of our house to make a kitchen area. We had old pots and pans, discarded empty food tins and we would make imaginary meals using the things which grew in the garden such as rhubarb, raspberries and of course, apples.

Like most siblings of different ages we were not at the same stage of mental development and so our games were frustrated by us having wildly different ideas about what the play house was for. My sister would be carefully making 'dinner' on the cardboard cooker whilst I climbed on the shelves in the tree, leaping off with Tarzan-like yells and sending the food tins flying. When a few years separate you, you are never really on the same page, despite often being thrown together to play.

We also had a play tent. It was a small wigwam with a red vinyl floor and yellow sides. It was held down on the ground with three long pegs. My dad didn't like the tent for three reasons. One was that it made pale, squashed patches on his lawn. He was a very keen gardener and took pride in his lawn. Secondly, we made holes in the lawn with the tent pegs. But what annoyed him the most was when we temporarily lost one of the three tent pegs. For some reason this used to make him really mad and we always got a big lecture about being careless and how tent pegs didn't grow on trees.

We played noisy games running in and out of the tent of course but my favourite times were when I played in the tent alone. I would sit quietly on a blanket on the floor, relishing the silence and revelling in being cocooned in the wigwam, peeking out at the world but safe within one of my own making.

## 22 ~ THE FRIED EGG

Despite being given a lot of responsibility early on there was one thing I never learned to do. Try as I might, I just couldn't cook. I was always afraid of burning myself on the hot pans or on the oven door and any attempts to create anything in the kitchen ended in failure.

My dad realised I was challenged in this department and gently coached me to the point where I could fry sausages. This was great because I loved sausage sandwiches. However, the fried egg long eluded me.

One day when I was well into my teens I decided I must conquer my fear of the egg. My sister had left home at this stage. On the day I decided to join the ranks of egg fryers I was alone in the house so I decided to ring her for instructions.

'Oh, It's easy,' she said casually. 'Break the egg into a cup first and have it ready. Then heat the fat, tip the egg gently in and scoop oil over it a few times with a spoon and the yolk will turn pink.'

'Yeah but the bit I don't understand is, how do you know when the oil is the right heat to put the egg in?'

'Well, you just kind of know.'

'I need more guidance than that. Are there any signs?'

'When the oil starts to bubble a bit, then put your egg in. Okay?'

'That's great. Thanks.'

I used up a few eggs to begin with as each egg I broke I managed to put my thumb right through. But eventually I managed to crack the shell open without harming the egg and into the cup it went. I was halfway there.

I began heating the oil, keeping a sharp eye out for bubbles. I knew that eggs tended to make the fat spit so I wound some tea towels around my arms. I had my spoon ready for the scooping part. It was a waiting game now.

After about twelve minutes by my kitchen clock the oil still hadn't produced a single bubble but there was a blue haze coming off the pan and a very strong kind of hot vibe around it. I even thought I detected a little smoke.

'Surely it's ready by now,' I thought. I decided to chance it. If the egg didn't cook I could always start again.

I tipped the egg into the pan.

What happened next I can only describe as an egg explosion. There was an amazing sound and general mayhem and before I could even get my spoon in position the egg was all over the walls. Luckily, I had kept my head well back so I didn't get boiling egg on my face. Well, maybe I did, figuratively speaking.

After I had cleaned up the mess I phoned my sister again and told her what had happened.

'Twelve minutes?' she shrieked! 'Are you a complete idiot?'

Apparently I was. I hung up with my tail between my legs and had a packet of crisps instead. Comfort food, you understand. And thankfully already fried.

## 23 ~ WANTING A PET

The thing I wanted most desperately as a young child was a pet. Preferably a dog. I envied every family I knew that had a dog. When I was still only about three feet tall I was being looked after by my mum's friend when she visited her elderly mother, taking me with her. I immediately wanted to befriend their rather scruffy dog but it obviously wasn't used to little folk and it began growling at me. I told my mum's friend.

'Our Suzie growled at you? No! She wouldn't hurt a fly. Gentle as a lamb, that dog.'

A few moments later the lamb-like dog took a chunk out of my lip. I had to be taken to hospital where the treatment included a hefty anti-tetanus jab. I wasn't one bit put off and continued to pet every dog I came across.

An old lady who lived across the road had a small, fat, long haired terrier with legs about three inches long. The lady called me over one day and asked me if I would try taking it for a walk. I was very happy to do so. I was proud to have a dog on the end of a lead to walk, even though it looked nothing like Scooby-Doo, my ideal pet. As I set off, the old lady shouted, 'make sure she has a bowel movement!' This made me go pink right up to my ears. I walked the dog every day for about two years. My reward was the pleasure of fantasising for a short while that this was really my own dog. The owner used to knock on the window and mime a vigorous running motion with her arms. She wanted it to lose weight. To please her I would jog until out of sight, but it was plain the poor old dog wasn't up to it, so mostly we just ambled along.

I begged for a pet of my own nearly every day. My mum bought me a clockwork mouse made of tin. I complained that pet mice lived in cages so she presented me with a rectangular casserole dish with a sprinkling of porridge oats covering the base to resemble sawdust. In one corner she placed a small pot of water and in another, a jam jar lid full of sunflower seeds. This kept me happy - for a while.

I had a goldfish next. It was called Mopsy and lived for nine years. I even spoke about it in my French exam at school, 'Il est un bon age pour un poisson rouge!' My sister and I were given a white rabbit each. Hers was called Snowy and mine was called Peter. My dad built elaborate hutches for them and a run surrounded by a six foot high wire fence. Unfortunately a neighbour's German shepherd dog (known as an Alsatian in those days) couldn't be kept from trying to get at the rabbits. One day we were inexplicably told that Peter and Snowy had gone to live on a farm.

When I was seven I was blessed with a dog of my own. He was a peculiar mix of a collie crossed with a corgi. He was black and tan with a long coat and short legs. I called him Mitch. He was an adorable puppy but as he matured it became obvious Mitch had a few problems with his temperament. It didn't matter to me. He was my best friend and we went everywhere together. I told him all my troubles and he always listened.

One awful day, five years later, Mitch turned on me, pinned me down and bit me on the chest. He stood over me, growling and snarling and my mum only managed to move him by banging a metal tea tray on her knees. Once again it was off to hospital with me but this time the consequences were more serious.

Our family had just acquired our first car, a Mini Clubman. My parents drove off, grave faced with Mitch on the back seat. They were going to consult with a vet to see what could be done about Mitch's vicious outbursts. My sister and I instinctively knew what could possibly happen. We knelt in her bedroom and began praying, making all sorts of bargains with God. Between prayers we rushed to the window, looking for the car. Eventually the Mini pulled up and Dad got out first. I could tell by his face that the news wasn't going to be good. Then Mum got out and they walked together up the Green without letting Mitch out of the car.

We strained to see into the back of the car from behind the musty net curtain. There was no little face peeking out of the car. We both realised at the same moment that the dreadful deed had already been done. My best friend was no more.

## 24 ~ THE LIBRARY

When I was a very young child in the 1960s there were almost no books in our house. My parents were not keen on reading so it didn't really occur to them to buy me books. I can only recall owning one toddler's book, *My Book of Manners*. It had pictures of animals in it performing social niceties such as putting on a napkin before a meal, with accompanying text explaining social etiquette. It doesn't sound like the most exciting children's book but I adored and treasured it. I had learned to read quite quickly in my infant school and I loved my new found ability to entertain myself and lose myself inside *My Book of Manners*.

At a very young age, something wonderful happened. A family friend who was babysitting me took me to the local library and enrolled me as a member. It was a tiny building with one (always female) member of staff. It smelled of floor polish and that unique smell that comes from old books.

I can remember being amazed at the idea that we would not have to pay for these books but could borrow them. It was impressed upon me that I had to take special care of them. Among the first books I borrowed were *Miffy at the Seaside* which had lots of strongly coloured pictures of a rabbit on the beach and *MacPherson* which was about a Scottish messenger boy.

You could borrow three or four books at a time and I practically flew home with my cache of wonderful books. They enhanced my small world so much. We were not bombarded with lots of toys in those days so this was a rare treat.

I was allowed to keep my cardboard membership card myself and because the library was only about half a mile away I was soon permitted to go there unaccompanied. I felt so grown up, going there alone and making my own choices.

My parents, seeing how much I enjoyed my library books, began to buy me books of my own and soon I had a bookcase full of them.

Thus began a love of books that has lasted my whole lifetime. My memories of the library are such happy ones. I wasn't constantly entertained the way children often are these days but with my library ticket I could enter any world I chose.

Reading so many books undoubtedly helped me develop my command of language and broadened my world to an incredible degree. I think it would be such a shame if libraries became a thing of the past. My local library now is in an old church, complete with stained glass windows and indoor balconies. It is a delightful place.

I would go as far as to say the library was the most important place I went to as a child. Going to Sunday school also shaped me but that was a rather passive experience. The library was different and through it I not only grew but learned a lot about myself.

No matter how much the world changes, let's hope we will always have libraries.

## 25 ~ ON THIN ICE

Ice skating was a very popular pastime for teenagers when I was young. I lived about an hour's bus ride away from a beautiful skating rink. Just seeing the ice sparkling under the lights gave me butterflies in my tummy. Skating at speed around the rink while holding hands with your friends was completely exhilarating.

We used to hire the boots from a booth by the changing rooms. It was pot luck whether you got a comfy pair or one with lumps and bumps that dug into you and made skating difficult. My sister was given a pair of skates by my parents but she wanted white ones and they were brown. She painted them with something so they ended up sort of flaky white.

A DJ in a fancy raised booth played records as we sped along. The rink was policed by youths in red coats who could skate like the wind. There was a photo booth inside the building and I still have some strips of snaps of my friends and I on skating trips.

My sister had a coat I greatly admired, which I think was called a trench coat. It made me think of something Nelson would have worn. It was calf length and very tight around the legs. It was Air Force blue, double breasted and had big lapels. I was skilled at picking her wardrobe lock and borrowed it a couple of times without her knowing. It fitted me like a glove and I fancied I looked stylish in it. But most of the time she was wearing it herself.

My mum noticed my admiration of the coat and tried to get me a similar one. However, the one she got was of a chunkier weave, was miles too big for me and horror of horrors - it was brown. I really dislike brown clothes. But I had to pretend to like the awful coat. When I pulled the belt tight around my waist it billowed out at the bottom, ruining the slim line look.

The first time I wore it skating I sulked. I had just turned thirteen. I was glad to hang the ghastly thing in my locker in the changing rooms and skate around in a warm jumper and my best jeans. I came off the ice, fairly tired as we all used to be after a long skating session, only to find someone had forced the locker door open and stolen my coat.

In the seventies any child damaging or losing clothing was always in massive trouble. 'You've ruined your good clothes' was a war cry we all came to dread. Losing something as expensive as a coat guaranteed there would be a fairly bad row ahead.

I'm sure you can guess what happened. My mum simply did not believe me that the coat had been stolen without any help from me.

'You've hated that coat from the beginning,' she raged. 'You lost it on purpose. You probably dumped it in some bin somewhere.' I can't remember what my punishment was but I certainly didn't get a replacement coat.

I've got to admit though, whoever stole it did me a huge favour.

## 26 ~ LATCHKEY KID

Like many of my generation, I was a latchkey kid. My mum returned to work when I was quite young and from then on I had to take a step up in responsibility.

I wore my front door key around my neck, on a piece of string, tucked under my clothing like a necklace. It was a Yale key and had been painted purple by the key cutter. I suppose that was the fashion at the time.

At 4 o'clock I would set off home from school and let myself into the empty house. I would light the gas fire, draw the curtains and put on the light. Next I would let the dog out and feed him. Then I would read my note which was always sitting propped up against the sugar bowl on the sky blue Formica kitchen table.

It was a standing joke in our house that my mum's writing was hard to read. She was always in a great hurry and pressed so hard on the paper with her Biro that the paper sometimes ripped. Important points were underlined, very heavily, several times for emphasis.

My note always started this way:

*Make cup of tea and have bag of crisps and three biscuits.*

This was her way of telling me not to have any MORE than three biscuits.

*Wash, dry and put away breakfast dishes. Take washing off pulley and fold. Use sweeper in L room and dust.*

We had a metal carpet sweeper instead of a vacuum cleaner which squeaked loudly when you pushed it.

*Do homework.*

It wasn't the warmest of welcomes after a hard day at school but daily chores were always a part of our lives as kids.
Mum would get home around 6pm and we would all watch *Crossroads* and then we'd have something simple for tea such as beans on toast.
I was often ill with tonsillitis and would be allowed to stay off school in a bed on the sofa. This was total luxury, watching educational programmes on TV, but a bit lonely all on my own. If I was really ill the lady next door would come in at lunchtime and heat me up some soup. She always sang the same song in a quavery voice while she heated my lunch. It went:

*Hey little hen. When, when, when will you lay me an egg for my tea?*

I would be left a bottle of Lucozade in the morning which I adored. Back then it was regarded as a drink for those who were ill. But it was very expensive so my mum would indicate a point on the label and say, 'you can have that much.' Medication was usually just a tube of Tunes throat sweets which also had to be rationed.

Sometimes when I was alone in the house things would crop up which I was not equipped to cope with. One day the gas fridge went wrong somehow and started pumping out fumes which smelled like ammonia. I ran to fetch a neighbour but he just popped his head in and said, 'that ain't right, Duck. I'd get out of here if I were you,' and left me to it.

One day my sister had come home early from school and hid upstairs in the bedroom with a large knife in her hand. She had arranged the lights so that her shadow cast in perfect detail on the landing wall and when I was about to go upstairs, I saw this terrifying knife wielding figure's shadow, moving ever so slightly.

Bizarrely, I tried to reason with the maniac, shouting from the bottom step of the stairs. I ordered 'him' to come downstairs and leave at once and promised that I wouldn't phone the police. The knife twitched a little in the shadows but the person did not move.

Losing my nerve suddenly I fled next door, shouting the name of the lady who lived there. My sister appeared behind me, bent double with laughter saying 'it was me you daft bat!'

I harboured a grudge about the terrible fright she had given me for years and got my revenge pulling a similar stunt when she was about fourteen. I pretended to be an intruder coming in the front door and she ran screaming out of the back door. I then had the satisfaction of watching her try to scale the six foot garden fence wearing high heeled platform shoes and a pencil skirt.

Kids can be really horrible to each other sometimes!

## 27 ~ COMMUNICATION

The one toy my sister and I both wanted more than anything when we were little was a set of walkie-talkies. I used to pretend to talk into one by using one of those metal tape measures coiled up in a square housing. I used to pull the 'antenna' up and run around the Green, dropping to my knees and speaking urgently into it.

It was such fun to make toy telephones from paper cups with a length of cotton as telephone wire. We were forever improving on previous designs. We always wanted to communicate between our bedrooms at night, but this meant leaving the cotton pulled taught across the landing where it would be in someone's way. We had to wait until the parents had gone to bed and then inevitably, one of us would have fallen asleep making it impossible to test the latest prototype.

Real phone calls were expensive. My mum put a telephone lock on our phone. You could still dial 999 in an emergency but that was all. It was a little metal barrel that fitted over one of the dialling holes. My sister was always desperate to ring her friends or boyfriend. I discovered I could pick this lock with a hair grip and used to charge her for doing so. Ten pence each time.

We also had a complicated device for calculating the cost of telephone calls which was plugged into the wall and sat underneath our telephone. My parents would phone far off places such as America to speak to our distant relatives. We would be allotted thirty seconds each to say hello and then we'd pass the phone to the next person. This device was hit by ball lightning and destroyed in 1980!

We didn't have electronic gadgets to play with as children do nowadays. One thing that fascinated us was the manual typewriter that my mum got second hand one day. It was black all over and incredibly heavy. It took two of us to carry it and lift it onto the dining table. It really seemed to have come out of the Ark. The keys travelled a long way down before they connected. You could choose between red and black print, by shifting the ribbon which we thought was fantastic. 'Ooh, red writing!'

My mum tried to make us learn proper typing by printing sentences that used all the letters of the keyboard or were a specific length.

*The quick brown fox jumped over the lazy dog.*

*Now is the time for all good men to come to the aid of the party.*

Of course, if you made a mistake, you had to take your paper out, carefully load a fresh sheet without letting it become crooked and start again.

Letter writing was a common way of communicating. At Christmas time we were always forced to spend Boxing Day writing thank you letters to relatives who had sent gifts.

*Dear Auntie,*

*Thank you so much for the lovely bath salts. I had a lovely bath last night and they made the water smell lovely.*

A lot of people had pen friends in other cities or countries. I always wanted a pen friend but somehow was never able to organise it.

Instead of the internet, the source of all knowledge was a set of encyclopedias. People came to the doors selling them all the time. We didn't have a set however, just a basic children's encyclopedia.

If you were doing a school project and you wanted some facts and figures you had to take the bus into town and go to the 'Big Library' where they had the encyclopedias you needed in their reference section.

One day I was about to set off for the library when my sister said, 'will you drop this book back for me while you are there?' I agreed and asked her to drop it in my bag along with mine as I was in a hurry.

The librarian began checking the books in and then stopped when she came to my sister's. She frowned and looked at me over her glasses. 'This book is two years overdue,' she said crossly. There will be a substantial fine. I blushed guiltily and realised I'd been had!

## 28 ~ BROWNIES

I was never really that keen to join the Brownie Guides. The main reason was that part of the uniform was a brown dress. I always hated the colour brown so I had never pictured myself as a Brownie. At the age of about eight, however, I will admit to having envied those wearing the yellow neckerchief thing which went with the Brownie outfit. It crossed over below the collar in a rather sophisticated way. The Cubs and Scouts had a much nicer uniform to my eye, with even more elaborate neck pieces but no amount of wishing would get me that uniform.

One day my mum suddenly announced that I was about to join the Brownies. Back in those days, if your mum told you that you were going to do something, you just did it. I was in a six called The Elves. My memory is a little fuzzy now but I think the other groups were called Pixies, Sprites and Kelpies.

Each group had a girl in charge who was called the Sixer. She looked after the tin with all our useful things in it such as pieces of string, a candle and some chalk. There was also a Seconder (I'm not sure of her specific role.) I was just an ordinary Brownie.

My first badge was the hostess badge for which I had to make Brown Owl a cup of tea and a sandwich. Being a latchkey kid, I was skilled at making tea but I was never much of a one for making anything edible in the kitchen, preferring crisps and other instant snacks. The bread ripped when I tried to butter it and the sandwich looked a little bit distressed. It went down quite well though. I was successful and I was proud of my badge.

For another badge, part of my job was to demonstrate that I could make a phone call from a telephone box. Brown Owl came with me to adjudicate. We traipsed to the row of shops and into the red telephone box where I had to ring Brown Owl's husband and relay a message, something about her being late home for tea. He thanked me and I hung up. Brown Owl told me I had passed and I heaved a sigh of relief.

I went on to join the Girl Guides when I was a little older. They had a blue uniform, which was slightly nicer but I always felt out of my depth as some of the girls there were so grown up they actually had bosoms and were about twice my height. These older girls ignored little newbies like me so it wasn't much fun.

Unfortunately we seemed to have a lot of solemn ceremonies in the Guides which often involved sitting in a circle around a lighted candle and being silent for several minutes. One of these ceremonies was a very serious affair, during which we were supposed to remember some long dead dignitary.

My only friend in Guides was a girl called Susan. She wasn't much older than me but was from a different school. She had straw coloured hair that stuck out in two bunches held in place with red 'bobbles' and a wide mouth that was always laughing. It was the laughing part that was my downfall that evening.

Susan was an expert at pulling funny faces. As we all sat in silence with the light off around this candle, I glanced sideways and she was making one of these unbelievably hilarious faces. My shoulders began to shake and she saw this and exploded with laughter, making me burst out laughing too.

We were immediately told to 'stop it at once' but we were helpless with mirth and could not get a grip of ourselves. Susan was sent out of the room and the respectful silence resumed. But only for a few seconds.

I could see Susan through the glass in the top part of the door. She looked at me, tilted her head to one side, crossed her eyes and raised her top lip, exposing what looked like buck teeth. This was too much for me altogether and I dissolved into a hysterical heap. The other Guides, sitting cross legged around me were not amused.

I was sent out too and when the lights went up we got the most terrible telling off. The next day our mothers were told we were no longer welcome at Guides as we were a disruptive influence.

I can't honestly say I was sorry. I had never really felt a part of things. Now I could go back to playing football with the neighbour's kids on summer evenings instead of being terribly earnest and girly. I don't know what became of Susan. I never saw her again.

## 29 ~ MUSIC

Mum and Dad liked music a lot and there was music playing in our house very frequently. My dad played guitar and sang and my mum would join in with her favourites. My dad had a lovely tenor voice.

He sang and played songs such as 'Jealous Heart', 'Nobody's Child', 'For These Are My Mountains' and 'Are You Lonesome Tonight?'

Their favourite song, in fact, 'their tune' was 'Put Your Sweet Lips a Little Closer to the Phone'. I think technically it was called 'He'll Have to Go'.

They had a lovely old mono record player. It was grey with Bakelite fittings and a cloth grille cover at the front. The turntable was a deep raspberry colour. You could stack several records up at once ready to play and each one would drop down onto the last one. I loved to watch this happen.

Their records varied quite a bit. 'These Boots are Made for Walking'. 'Georgy Girl'. 'A World of Our Own'.

I had three party pieces I sang with my Sooty guitar and with my red bobbled Singing Hat on. 'These Boots are Made for Walking', 'Little Arrows' and when I was slightly older, 'Ernie'.

They had LPs by Des O'Connor, Val Doonican, The Bachelors and my favourite, Miki and Griff.

I was often confused by love songs and tended to take lyrics literally. I would lie on the orange and brown leaf patterned carpet watching the record oscillate slightly as it spun around. Tom Jones sang about a girl called Mary who he seemed to like a lot on a song called 'Green Green Grass of Home'. He described her in the lyrics as having *hair of gold and lips like cherries*. I imagined Mary with a shining metallic bobbed hairdo and completely round lips. Another man who sang about lips was Englebert Humperdinck on his song 'Release Me'. *Her lips are warm while yours are cold*. I imagined a woman with freezing lips had him imprisoned behind bars. I felt sorry for her that he didn't want her just because her mouth was on the cold side.

My parents adored Jim Reeves and there was one particular album of his they played all the time when I was very small. It had a song on it called 'I Won't Forget You'. It included a line that went *Though you don't want me now, I'll still love you. Till the breath in my body has gone.*

Jim sang the word 'body' in a funny accent. I thought he was singing the word 'budgie' and used to picture a budgerigar gasping its last breath. The mental picture could bring tears to my eyes. What a sad song.

If I had to pick just one song that reminds me of those times it would be Miki and Griff's 1963 hit, 'I Want to Stay Here'.

## 30 ~ I CAN AND I WILL

When I was fourteen, I began to really struggle with something that was to affect me for the rest of my life. Social anxiety. It wasn't called that then. It was just called 'being shy.' Later on I would develop full blown agoraphobia as well but for the time being, in the mid 1970s, all I knew was that my shyness was getting worse and worse.

Walking to school, I would get more and more anxious. My school had 1200 pupils and wasn't for the faint-hearted. I would sweat and tremble and my stomach would churn and I had to fight the urge to flee the nearer I got to the big school gates. What was more, I was deeply ashamed of my extreme shyness and was afraid to tell anyone about it. I had a secret dread that one day, total panic would overwhelm me and I would become paralysed with fear.

One day, I was reading the newspaper, when I saw a small headline in the advertisements section. 'Are you shy?' it asked. 'Do you have problems talking to people? Do you lack confidence?' I mentally ticked all the boxes as I read on. 'Send now for our free booklet, *I Can and I Will*' and learn how to banish shyness forever.' My mum walked by and I quickly turned the page. Sneaking the paper into my bedroom, I copied out the London address. The booklet would come in a plain brown wrapper, it said. I was always first up and collected the post so nobody need ever find out. I quickly wrote out my address and sent it off.

I watched the doormat carefully for an unfamiliar envelope every day until at last it came. I ripped open the envelope and inside was a small yellow booklet entitled, *I Can and I Will*. This was it! This was the answer to all my problems. I was late for school but kept pulling it out of my blazer pocket as I hurried along to sneak glances inside.

The booklet was a terrible disappointment. It was full of testimonials from satisfied customers who had sent off forty-two pounds and enrolled in their correspondence course all about how to overcome shyness. Mrs J from Cardiff said she had once been a nervous wreck but was now running her own company. Mr C from Aberdeen said his social life was now so busy he could hardly remember the frightened man he had once been.

The strange thing was, I actually had forty-two pounds. It was a lot of money in those days. But I had been saving pocket money, birthday money and every penny I could get for a stereo record player for a long time. I did not hesitate to run to the shops at the earliest opportunity to buy a postal order and send it off.

The course itself was a bit baffling. It came in eight booklets and talked a lot about the subconscious mind, breathing correctly, and something they called 'auto suggestion.' There were a lot of visualisation exercises. I kept skipping forward to the end of each booklet. Where was the bit that would tell me how to get to the school Christmas party without being consumed by nerves? I had no private place to keep anything like this, so I put the booklets under the carpet. There was a slight bump but hopefully no one would notice.

One day, I came home from school and my mother was waiting with the booklets in her hand. She was angry. Where had I got the money for this rubbish? When she found out I had spent my stereo money she nearly exploded. Forty-two pounds? Was I mad? How dare I make a decision like that without consulting her and my father. They were very disappointed in me. I had shown myself to be untruthful. Nothing was said about the fact that I was struggling badly just to make it to school every day although I did try to explain. It was all nonsense, she said angrily.

The course did help me a little bit, for a while. One of the exercises was to join a local sports or hobbies club. I drew upon my small reserves of courage and joined a karate club. I also made a new friend around this time and became a little happier.

Looking back, when I think of this time in my life, I feel sad that when I was little more than a child, I had nowhere to turn but to a newspaper advert that promised the world and delivered so little. I was trying to deal with a complex problem all alone. It was to become a lifelong battle but fortunately I now have a wonderful, supportive person in my life to listen to my fears and cheer me on.

I don't blame my parents for reacting the way they did. It was all outside of their understanding and they obviously thought by dismissing it as 'nonsense' it would go away. Life was often a struggle for working class people and they had no time to indulge anyone who was being shy. You squared up to life and you got on with it.

## 31 ~ RECORDS

I can remember the moment when music first tugged at my heart strings and grabbed a hold of my soul. It was the summer of 1971 and I was eight years old. I was sitting in the house of one of my sister's friends, on the sofa drinking tea. Another friend of hers was there as well, and my sister herself. The four of us sat listening as the oldest of the group selected records and played them on the old mono record player.

Suddenly a song began with such an emotive melody that my eyes filled up with tears. The lyrics told a story. As the older girls chatted I listened to the words drifting from the speaker. It was a very sad story. The singer was the legendary Diana Ross who was just twenty-seven at the time and the song was the classic, 'I'm Still Waiting'.

I was by far the youngest there that day. My sister had probably been instructed to take me along by my mum as it was the school holidays. So I really had no say in what we did but I spoke up anyway as the song came to an end. 'Can we have that one on again?' Nobody objected. The song stayed with me for a long time.

The Piglets' song 'Johnny Reggae' was the next record I loved. Then when I was nine I heard the most beautiful song, performed by an angel faced boy with the purest of voices who was only just turning fourteen. The boy was Michael Jackson and the song was 'Ain't No Sunshine'. It was the first record I went out and bought for myself. It remained my all time number one record for many years to come.

At the beginning of my tenth birthday party, a boy from my class called Russell gave me 'How Can I Be Sure?' by the gorgeous David Cassidy, all wrapped up with a bow on top. I was taken aback at what was then judged to be a very expensive gift. This particular 45 was warped which was a common flaw among records in those days. I still played it until it almost disintegrated, watching it rise and fall as it turned.

'Let's Dance' by Chris Montez was another song that I adored in that year of 1972. When I was twelve, three years later the Bay City Rollers released a smoochy single called 'Give A Little Love'. The B side was a song called 'She'll be Crying Over You'. This rang out through my bedroom door for months, if not years to come.

The most popular place to go for those of us of eleven years old and older was the local kid's disco. It took place on the fourth Friday of every month. It was talked about endlessly - who was going, what we were going to wear, who would call for whom on the way there. The DJ was a local guy with long hair and fuzzy sideburns. His favourite song was 'The Liquidator' by The Harry J Allstars. It became the theme tune of the disco and was a guaranteed floor filler. There was a funny dance that went with it where you moved as if your legs had become jelly but kept your feet still. You were not supposed to smile while you danced. It was fashionable to gaze into the distance with a moody stare. But we were all having the time of our lives.

These songs were the soundtrack to my childhood. Any one of them can transport me back to the early seventies. A time when my friends and I were so eager to dance to them that we ran hand in hand to the middle of the dance floor, whooping with joy and shouting, 'this is my favourite!'

## 32 ~ PONY MAD

One of the most fabulous holidays I ever went on was a pony trekking holiday to Wales in 1976. I had begun learning to ride a year earlier and like a lot of girls my age was pony mad.

We travelled there in a van. The journey was several hours on a motorway and there were no seats in the rear of the vehicle. We simply sat on the floor in the back and sang songs all the way.

The horses came with us from the riding school in a horse lorry, so we knew all of them personally. We had been told before we left that we would each be assigned a horse for the entire week. All I could think of as we bumped along in the van was, 'I hope I get Boxer!'

I didn't get my favourite horse. As we were going to be on horseback for many hours each day it was important that the heavier people got the bigger horses. I weighed about seven stone wet through at the age of thirteen and so I was given a tiny skewbald mare called Poppet. She was not much more than twelve hands high.

Being away from your parents in new surroundings at a young age is quite thrilling. We stayed in a falling down old farmhouse with a chemical toilet in the field behind it. It had no hot water. We just sloshed our faces with cold water for a wash every morning.

Each of us was responsible for our assigned pony. At first light each day we had to catch it in the field half a mile away, walk it back to the farmhouse, groom it and put on the tack we had cleaned. Then we rode for miles in a group, dismounting somewhere scenic for lunch and then trekking back.

There were no beds. We slept in large bedrooms in sleeping bags on the floor. One night we were whispering and giggling as only thirteen year old girls can. Some of us decided to walk the lanes in the dark and visit the horses' field to see if it was true that they slept standing up. A few less adventurous ones stayed behind.

We walked by torchlight but it was still really scary. When we got to the field, the horses were standing quite far off so we couldn't see if they were asleep or not. We headed back only to discover that one of the group who had remained had locked us out.

I pried open the tiny window above the main kitchen window and slithered in headfirst. Unfortunately the draining board of the sink was covered in cutlery which I landed on, scattering it everywhere. It made a heck of a noise.

Our teacher was furious and we had one of those lecture that goes, 'you've let your school down, you've let me down and most of all you've let yourself down.'

There was one boy in the group. He had a double-barrelled surname and was terribly posh. He was constantly scathing about the rest of us and our riding skills and inferior mounts. He had brought his own horse in a swanky horse box. Eventually we had taken all the snooty remarks we could take. We had all saved our best clothes for the gymkhana which was to take place on the last day. We stole his carefully pressed best jodhpurs, put them in a tree and hurled mud at them. He had to ride in jeans on the big day.

I entered a trotting race and won my heat. In the final I was against the posh lad and another girl on a big horse. My little pony was a mighty trotter and was winning easily. But I had forgotten to do up my girth properly and my saddle began to slip as I approached the finish line. As I slid sideways the other two sailed past me. I finished up almost under Poppet's belly but clung on and was awarded a yellow rosette.

A gold medal couldn't have thrilled me more and it had pride of place in my bedroom for a long time to come.

## 33 ~ LETTING THE WORLD IN

When I was five, a very exciting thing happened at home. Our first telephone was installed. It was a large, green, two tone device. There was only one phone socket, right next to the front door so we could only make calls in the hall. My dad built a very complicated telephone stand for it out of dark coloured, deeply grained wood. This consisted of three tiers. The phone was on the top shelf, address books, pens and a pad sat on the middle level, and the massive, heavy phone directories lay at the bottom.

Our hall was usually freezing with a fair sized draught blowing through the gaps around the front door. When talking on the phone, you had to either stand or sit on the bottom step of the stairs. The whole thing wasn't a very comfortable experience but nevertheless we considered ourselves very lucky.

We weren't the only people using our line, however. We were on a thing called a party line which meant that someone else in another location shared our telephone line, and the two of us couldn't use it at the same time. For some strange reason, this person wasn't even in our road, but in a block of flats in the next street. If we were already talking and she picked up her handset, she could hear every word of our conversation. She would often interrupt and say, 'can you hurry up? I need to make an important call.' If we didn't hang up straight away she would sit listening until we were obliged to capitulate.

The new phone enabled us to talk to the many relatives we had all over the world. But one day we realised, in quite a shocking way, that it also let the world into our home.

I was six and my sister eight when it happened. We were home alone, which would be scandalous by today's standards but seemed pretty normal then. Our parents were both at work. The phone rang and I raced to answer it. A man's voice asked if my father was in. I said no. Was anyone else in, he wanted to know. I said my big sister was there. He told me to put her on. I yelled for her and she came to the phone. I pressed my ear next to hers so I could hear what was going on. It wasn't every day we got phone calls.

'I want you to listen very carefully,' the voice said slowly. 'Your mother won't be coming home tonight. She's been kidnapped.' And he hung up.

We began to sob hysterically and falling over each other we tumbled out of the door and ran to the next door neighbour's house. We began pounding on the door and screaming the name of the lady who lived there. Somehow, we managed to convey what had happened. The neighbour began to assure us our mum was fine and at work. But we would accept nothing less than to see her in person straight away.

Our mother worked a mile away, up a huge hill. I can still remember trying to keep up with the neighbour and my sister as I trailed along in great distress. I was still in my pyjamas. The neighbour hadn't thought to get me changed into outdoor clothes.

My mum was serving meals in the canteen where she worked when this unlikely trio arrived, my sister and I flinging ourselves at her legs and crying even harder.

Later, back at home, a kindly policeman and policewoman tried to reassure us about what was now referred to as The Hoax Phone Call. They never found out who it was. For a long time afterwards we flinched when the phone rang. And of course, the events of that day are as vivid to me now as they were then. Installing a telephone had given us access to the world. But it had also let the world in. A world which is sometimes a very scary place.

## 34 ~ CARS

I loved to play with toy cars from an early age. My favourite were called Matchbox cars. I would spend my pocket money on a different one every week and ended up with a decent little collection. In the local toyshop the cars were displayed in a glass cabinet. I spent a lot of time in there, just gazing at them and thinking about which one I would buy the following week. I wasn't often in a car myself. We walked everywhere or we went on buses and very occasionally we would go somewhere by train.

I liked to sit on the top deck of the bus. I loved it when the tree branches scraped the roof. One winter when I was very little our bus broke down in deep snow. We were nearly a mile from home. The driver got out and went to the back of the vehicle and produced several shovels. All the male passengers got off and began to dig snow from around the wheels but it didn't work. So my mum and I began to walk home. It seemed a really exciting adventure, holding her hand tightly as we carefully made our way through this new white wonderland.

Not many ordinary working class people had cars in the sixties or early seventies. We didn't get our first car until I was eleven. We got an old blue Mini Clubman and not long after that we got a bright red Hillman Imp, a car that I grew to have a love-hate relationship with. One thing the Imp was very bad at was starting. The problem was traced at various times to all sorts of parts but to save getting technical I'll just say that my dad, who was not very mechanically minded, always blamed the battery.

We could not afford a new battery so he had this idea that the battery should be charged every evening and carried down and reattached ready for starting the car in the morning. We had a kind of council green semicircle in front of our house that you weren't allowed to drive on so this required carrying the heavy battery up and down the hill twice a day. My dad had a sort of fixation that the battery was dangerous and that us kids might touch it while it was charging so he always placed it where he could keep an eye on it as it charged every evening.

This 'safe' place was right in front of our gas fire which would be blazing away every night, next to his chair. I never thought anything strange about this until after I grew up when I mentioned to someone that I could never get near the fire because of the car battery always having pride of place. My friend gasped and told me that car batteries give off fumes when they are charging and should never be placed anywhere near a naked flame!

The council provided rows of garages for motorists who wanted them. My dad was delighted to get one even though it was a good half mile from the house. When I learned to drive I naturally wanted to use the car to comfortably travel from door to door. This wasn't allowed however as he didn't like the car sitting outside overnight when it might rain. I had to maneuver it into the garage, which was a hard enough job, dry it all over and then walk home! On the odd occasion I failed to do this he would glance out of the window and say crossly, 'look at that car out there in the rain, it'll be rotten with rust by the morning'!

## 35 ~ AMERICA

My dad was one of eight children who had spread out all over the globe to places like Australia, New Zealand and America. He had two sisters living in the States and the large family of another sister who had passed away. They hadn't seen each other for many years so one day it was decided that my folks should go on a holiday to America. Us kids were not going, just them.

Flights were very expensive. My mum had never been on a plane in her life and my dad had only been on planes while serving in World War Two. So needless to say they were very excited.

To pay for this, my mum got an extra job cleaning for a lady who lived about two miles away. My mum and this lady got on very well and became friends in the end. The extra money was carefully saved every week and by the summer of 1977 they had almost enough. Then a terrible thing happened.

It was the school summer holidays so I was at home. My mum and sister were at work. My dad had completed his morning shift at the factory and was lying on the couch. He had been very grumpy since he came home. Out of the blue he said he wasn't feeling well and told me to fetch the man next door but one.

I knew it was serious for three reasons. Firstly, he didn't particularly get on with this man. Secondly he was clutching his chest. And most frighteningly of all, his lips had gone blue.

A couple of hours later my mum, my sister and I were being led into my dad's hospital room by a nurse.

He was bare chested with the blankets up to his waist and he had wires attached to his chest and a tube in his nose. There were machines by the bed. My dad had had a heart attack.

We were only allowed to see him for a few minutes. He looked very sad. As we said goodbye he said, 'I love you' to us all and a tear ran down his cheek. I knew he was thinking he would never see us again. I had never heard him say he loved me. And I had never before seen him cry.

I had just bought a double LP by the Jackson Five. I spent a lot of time in my room listening to it. In particular I played a song called 'Daddy's Home' a lot. I've never played it since.

Thank God, Dad recovered. He had grown a moustache while he was in hospital which didn't suit him. He had to quit his 60 roll ups a day smoking habit and so for the first time in his life he grew slightly chubby. He was incredibly tetchy and moody but we had been told this was all part of it.

He was given strict instructions on what to do and what not to do during the recovery period. One of those things was no flying.

After being given this news, my mum went out and spent a large chunk of the saved, hard earned money on a big colour TV. It must have seemed a very poor substitute for the planned family reunion. But we were all just glad that we still had Dad.

## 36 ~ ENTERTAINMENT

Two really important events in our household were the *Eurovision Song Contest* and *Miss World*, which we watched on our black and white television set. Both competitions seemed terribly glamorous to us. Everyone talked about them the next day.

One Year the *Eurovision Song Contest* seemed particularly special. It was spring 1970 and I was seven and a half. We chose our places on the couch and as usual got ready with our pens and paper to mark each entry. We always had a small box of Milk Tray Chocolates to share for this event, as it only happened once a year. My sister always had the lime barrel, I had the strawberry one, Dad had the coconut diamond and Mum chose the hazelnut whirl.

This year we had to choose between two very pretty, smiling young women. Dana was singing Ireland's entry. It was a lilting melody called 'All Kinds of Everything'. She was only 18 years old. The other performance we loved was Mary Hopkin, representing Great Britain, singing 'Knock Knock, Who's There?' Mary was just 19.

Dana wore a short white dress and Mary a long dark one. The first girl was dark haired and the second a blonde.

'I want Mary Hopkin and Dana to win,' I declared confidently when all the entrants had performed.

'You can't have both,' my sister explained. 'You have to choose.'

I was on the horns of a dilemma for one of the first times in my life. Eventually I decided on Dana. Her song just had the edge. It was a good choice. Dana won and Mary Hopkin came second.

We didn't go to the theatre very often but I did once go on an outing organised by the factory my dad worked for. All the kids went on a bus to see *Toad of Toad Hall* performed. I liked the animal outfits but I must have been very young as I didn't understand any of it. Afterwards we met Santa and were each given a present. I was probably about four. I was given a *Collins English Dictionary* which, like the performance, was rather advanced for me.

Going to the cinema was considered a fabulous day out. I saw a few classic films with my mum, as a young child. *Fiddler on the Roof* was one and *Doctor Zhivago* another. I didn't really understand what was going on in those two movies but *Oliver!* was different. I was quite mesmerised by this film. The scenes with so many people singing and dancing in a sunny street were amazing. I was very frightened by the bit where Oliver Reed's character sends Oliver up onto the roof.

I also saw *Doctor Dolittle, The Sound of Music, Lady and the Tramp* and many others. The one that really captured my attention though was the musical film *Seven Brides for Seven Brothers*. I had no interest in the billowing dresses of the brides but wished so much that I was one of the brothers in their different coloured shirts as they leaped and bounded all over the screen. The displays of gymnastics and wonderful dancing in the barn raising dance scene inspired me to want to do it too. When I went home I spent ages practising jumping from the kitchen table, to a chair, to the floor and back up again with my arms spread wide, kicking my legs out as I went.

## 37 ~ UNDERWATER SEA DIVING

One of the delights of childhood is discovering new things for the first time. Simple things fascinated and pleased us back in those days. One of those new and interesting things that came into my life as a child was a sleeping bag.

We had an aunt, uncle and cousins coming to visit from a long way away and as we only had a three-bedroomed house it was decided some of us younger kids would sleep in the living room in sleeping bags.

It could be said that the colour of those sleeping bags eventually caused the accident that followed. Mine was royal blue and my sister's was a sort of aquamarine shade. They seemed massive to us and what really fascinated us was that you could zip them together and make one enormous double sleeping bag. What we liked about this was that when you went under the covers it was like being in a vast world of blue. In fact it was just like being under the sea.

At the time we got these sleeping bags, I had a friend called Sarah and we were always thinking up imaginative games to play. One of the best of these was 'underwater sea diving'.

We made diving suits out of black tights, complete with diving helmets. We had one real pair of flippers between us. I also had a proper diving face mask so we were well kitted out.

The sleeping bags were zipped together and placed on my bedroom carpet to represent the sea. We put shells inside and paper fish and we 'dived' between the layers with torches retrieving treasure. My bed represented the boat. My wooden stilts were oars. Part of the game involved having a picnic lunch on 'the boat' which consisted of pick and mix sweets in a large paper bag. We also had plastic cups and being quite quaint kids we had a flask of boiling water to make tea, along with a small bottle of milk and teabags. To be honest, eating the 'lunch' was the best part of the game so after a few quick dives we would sit on 'the boat' and tuck in.

One day we were home alone playing 'underwater sea diving' and it quickly got to the picnic lunch part. Clad in black tights from head to toe we sat on my bed and I held the two plastic cups while Sarah poured boiling water into them. The two of us were always giggling. She was making little noises of effort lifting the heavy flask and this made me laugh. Soon we were both laughing. As cups and flask jiggled about while we poured, a little boiling water landed on my hand.

'Ow!' I jerked up my hand in pain and before we knew what had happened most of the water from the flask was all over my legs. My sister came back from playing at her friend's house just at the right moment. My dad was at work and my mum was on the bus travelling back from work so my sister called her friend's mother. This lady told me to stand in the bath with cold water running on my legs. However, a few minutes had passed by now and when I took the tights off, I could see my legs were in a bad way.

My mum came home while I was standing in the bath, still wearing my nylon helmet and other diving clothes. Sarah and I were giggling again at this stage, not realising the seriousness of it.

More instructions from the friend's mother told us to wrap my legs in sheets (that part really hurt) and I went to hospital in a neighbour's Volkswagen Beetle. When the sheets came off, I could see the huge blisters. I had second degree burns, they said. I had to have my legs redressed every day for quite a long time.

That was the end of underwater sea diving. But I soon found another use for my sleeping bag. It was made of very slippery material. It made a fantastic bobsleigh if you climbed inside and launched yourself down the stairs, headfirst, arms outstretched to prevent smashing through the front door at the end of the hall.

## 38 ~ FOOD

One task I really enjoyed as a youngster was shelling peas for my mum. I was not yet at school when I began doing this job. She would get me to sit on the steps in the garden and would place a tray on my lap. On the tray, there would be a colander full of pea pods and an empty saucepan.

It seemed that the sun was always shining when I was busy doing this, in the way that all summers of our youth are remembered as glorious. Carefully, I would run my thumb down the pod, revealing the fresh green peas inside and then into the pot they would go.

We grew a lot of our own food back then as my dad was a keen gardener and we had a very large garden. Apples, rhubarb, raspberries, cabbages, cauliflower and strawberries, to name but a few, all sprouted in our soil.

My favourite was the strawberries. In the long, hot summer of 1976 we had a bumper crop of enormous, beautifully ripe strawberries. We were eating them morning, noon and night and any visitors to the house during that period were greeted with the words, 'would you like some strawberries?'

My dad also grew sweet peas. They remain my favourite flowers to this day. They had a beautiful scent and grew in such delicate shades of pink, lavender and white. We were encouraged to pick them and the house would be festooned with little bunches of them.

We had hot oat cereal for breakfast in the winter (the one that makes you glow with an orange outline in the TV advertisement) and ate cereal and cold milk in the summer. Boxes of cereal used to have fantastic free gifts inside. Sometimes you would get plastic figures to play with or stickers. I was supposed to wait until the gift appeared in the box but invariably, I had my little hand rammed to the bottom of the box, feeling around among the cereal for my toy.

Once I saved up tokens and sent away for a yellow and red, battery operated, plastic submarine. It was a wonderful thing with adjustable fins that would make it dive, surface or swim along just beneath the surface of my bath water.

On special occasions such as Mother's Day or my mum's birthday we would make her breakfast in bed. As little children it would take us ages to get everything ready and we would generally leave the toast and tea sitting there growing cold while we picked daisies to go in an egg cup beside the tray. This would be accompanied by carefully crayoned home made cards and a small gift.

One time I was sent to the local grocer shop to buy a sponge cake. I had to walk instead of cycling as it would require careful carrying. The cake came in a white cardboard box. We were all keen for a peep at the cake so we gathered around as my mum lifted the lid of the box as it sat on the kitchen table.

We all recoiled in horror as the cake came into view with hundreds of ants running all over it.

My mum had the art of returning shoddy or substandard foodstuffs down to a T. She was particularly fussy that meat should not be fatty or hard to chew. Picture our family as we sat down to Sunday dinner, all desperately trying to chew some very fatty meat as part of our meal. 'Is it fatty?' she would suddenly ask as our jaws tired. Before we had a chance to answer she would burst out with 'right then!' Our plates were grabbed and all the nasty meat was scraped into a see-through plastic bag and placed in the fridge. On Monday morning, my mum would march down to the butcher's, towing me behind her, sail to the front of the queue, slam the bag down on the counter and utter the immortal words, 'WOULD YOU EAT THAT?' She always got her money back!

## 39 ~ THE MAGIC T-SHIRT

My favourite memory is a very small moment out of a whole childhood but I can still remember how I felt; supremely happy. I was probably about seven years old so it would have been the summer of 1970. I worshiped my father but very much from afar as he was a very quiet hardworking man who didn't interact much with us children.

That summer, my mum bought him a navy blue T shirt with a white ring and a red ring around the crew neck. I don't know what you call the material but it was a sort of open weave in little squares, like gym shirts we had at senior school. Like piqué on a polo shirt. Anyway, I thought this T shirt was fabulous. My dad was my hero and I wanted to be just like him.

The following day I was playing outdoors on the semi circle of communal grass, called the Green, outside our house. The grass had just been cut by a man on the council ride-on mower, leaving patterns of heaped up grass behind in ridges. The family next door had seven children and the one next door but one on the other side had eight. We all used to come running out of our houses when the grass had been cut. Hordes of us throwing the grass in the air and running about, getting over excited. I guess children were easily pleased back then.

I saw my mum coming up the path from the bus stop with bags of shopping. She called me in and handed me a brightly coloured paper bag. Inside was a small navy blue T shirt exactly the same as my dad's. It had the white and red collar and the same textured weave. It fitted me like a glove. It was just perfect.

I was rendered pretty near speechless, because the gift was so unexpected, and it never occurred to me that a mini version of my dad's T shirt existed. I think I turned scarlet and said 'ooh, Thank you!' The other amazing thing was that I was allowed to wear it right away. I didn't have to save it 'for best.'

I went running outside again to join the other kids playing with the grass in the sunshine and I felt ten feet tall. I was so proud of my T shirt I could have burst. It was a moment of perfect joy.

I don't have any photographs of me wearing the fabulous T shirt but I still remember it vividly in my mind's eye and the invincible feeling I had wearing it.

## 40 ~ THE CHRISTMAS PREVIEW

Now that I've experienced Christmas over fifty times it has lost some of its original charm and appeal. I know some people adore the festivities but I do find the idea of repeating the same traditions year in, year out a little tedious. There's also the pressure to be exceedingly cheerful on the day. However, I haven't forgotten just how magical Christmas was as a young child.

My parents often spoke of their Christmases gone by. My dad said he was given a penny and my mum received an orange, some nuts and a pair of knitted gloves. By comparison, my sister and I were wildly spoiled every twenty-fifth of December.

We would wake up around four in the morning, feeling sick with excitement at the prospect of the present opening that was about to happen. We were always given a fixed time before which we were not allowed to wake our parents. As time crawled by, we resorted to counting the seconds out loud.

Finally the clock would reach the magic hour and we would race into Mum and Dad's bedroom, our shrill voices chattering nineteen to the dozen. My dad would be unbearably slow getting out of bed, putting his slippers and dressing gown on and sipping his tea. Once we were all downstairs, the rule was that we had to have a small breakfast of tea and toast to 'settle our stomachs.'

First we would give our parents their presents from us. Usually socks or a tie for Dad and *Oil of Ulay* for Mum. They were always gracious enough to look surprised and delighted. Then we would open the presents around the tree which were from aunts and uncles and from each other. Aged nine, I gave my sister a record called 'Coz I Luv You' by Slade. I put it into an empty Reddy Brek packet before wrapping it, which I thought was incredibly clever. 'She'll never guess what it is!' She bought me 'Johnny Reggae' by the Piglets. We then went to work on our stocking. This was one of Mum's American Tan coloured nylon stockings which bulged with cheap plastic toys. Finally we delved into The Sack - a pillow case stuffed with more substantial presents. This was all carried out in a frenzy of excitement.

One year this all went horribly wrong. At the age of seven, I had been told by a school teacher that Santa did not exist. My parents were furious. So I became obsessed with finding out where they were hiding my presents. Presumably it was at someone else's house as I never found any except on this one Christmas Eve.

Mum and Dad were happily watching something festive on the television so I sneaked into their bedroom in my bare feet to see if I could see any presents. It was about my hundredth trip in there to look that December. This time I hit the jackpot. Their eiderdown was loosely pulled up over a whole bed-load of bulky objects. When I pulled the cover back, there were all my presents, along with my sister's waiting to be wrapped. Wow!

I spent a good twenty minutes in there examining everything and then carefully replaced the eiderdown, sneaked out and went back downstairs, trying to act normal. I had a funny feeling that was more than just guilt. It was the feeling you get when it begins to dawn on you that you might have just made a big mistake.

As I sat on my sister's bed counting the seconds out loud as usual at about four o'clock the next morning, things just didn't feel the same as other years. I wasn't excitedly wondering what I had got. It was, in a way, all over before it had started.

But worse was to come. When it came time to open the sack, I recognised the shape of each wrapped present and already knew what was inside. The rectangular box was my new football boots. The soft square flat package was the black shirt I'd wanted so much. I had to feign surprise for the benefit of my beaming parents.

'Ooh football boots! I didn't expect this!'

The consequences of having to act out fake surprise for the best part of an hour had a far greater effect on me than the small amount of guilt I had felt during the peeking the night before. I felt like a massive fraud, like a total heel and of course I realised that I had ruined the wonder of Christmas for myself too.

I was about eight years old but I learned a valuable lesson. Never again have I been even slightly tempted to peek at a present.

## 41 ~ BRIDESMAID

It was considered a real honour to be asked to be a bridesmaid. I had never thought about it and we didn't know anyone who was getting married anyway so it never crossed my mind I might ever be one.

One day, my mum came rushing in from the hall with exciting news. Our Australian cousin was getting married and she wanted my sister and I as bridesmaids. 'We're going to Australia?' We looked at each other, growing excited. I immediately thought I might meet Skippy the Bush Kangaroo.

'No, she is flying over and getting married here. She's marrying a sailor who lives here.'

I didn't honestly really know what being a bridesmaid entailed, as I was only seven and had never been to a wedding.

I have a colour photo of us in our homemade bridesmaids dresses. The colour of the outfit is extraordinary. Think of the deepest pink you can possibly get and then add deep purple to the mix. The dresses were covered in glittery, sparkly bits; sort of like sequins. And then we had an Alice band each in our hair which had deep pink flowers on it.

We went to meet my cousin at the nearest airport. I had never been to an airport before and in fact was twenty before I got to board a plane myself. This lady seemed so glamorous to me. She was tall, slim and very pretty with a kind of beehive of jet black hair piled high on her head. When she got off the plane we admired her tan and clamoured to hold her hand and talk to her.

I don't remember too much about the wedding but two things stick in my mind. The best man was falling-over-drunk at the reception and I was really scared of this. I had never seen anyone drunk before. Also, I was required to have some photos taken by myself and the beginnings of shyness were taking hold, because I didn't like the attention.

When I was nine we were asked to be bridesmaids again. This time it was to a distant cousin who was getting married near London. The bride's grown up sister was to be matron of honour. She was an air hostess so she was another person we thought very sophisticated and glamorous.

I didn't enjoy the long session at the hairdressers where they tried to tease my short hair over the headdress. Our dresses were a very bright sky blue this time. The ceremony was incredibly long and we had to stand all the way through. It was a very hot day in July. The church seemed airless and the temperature was well into the eighties. I began to feel light headed and I could feel sweat running down my back. I only just made it through the wedding and had to lie down afterwards until the woozy feeling wore off.

At the end of the seventies I was my sister's bridesmaid. She got married very young on a freezing February day. Her best friend was the other bridesmaid. This time the dresses were a very subtle shade of pale pink.

I remember thinking that when I got married I would dispense with all the pomp and ceremony. The guests would wear jeans, we would all sit on beanbags on the floor and drink tea and eat chips and egg.

And did I have a wedding like that? Well, that is for another book!

## 42 ~ FLAMINGOS

As my sixteenth birthday dawned, I had a friend who was a boy, who had designs on becoming an actual boyfriend. He was two years older than me. He was in the upper sixth at school and as he lived a few streets away from me we used to walk to school together.

On my birthday he told me to get dressed up 'smartly' as we were going somewhere for a surprise. He also presented me with a fancy, blue, slim cigarette lighter so my parents now officially knew I smoked. (I quit a decade ago, but back then ALL teenagers smoked.)

Instead of going on the bus, we actually went into town in a taxi. He was really pushing the boat out! He had whispered the destination to the driver. My stomach flip flopped when it pulled up outside a small restaurant called *Flamingos* because in my whole sixteen years I had never eaten in a restaurant before. The prospect scared me to death because, like the rest of my family, I thought only posh people ate in restaurants. Thus I felt woefully out of my depth. I had been to cafés plenty of times, for chips and beans from the children's menu, but this was a whole different ball game.

We went in and he confidently gave his name as he had booked a table. I glanced quickly around and saw 'posh people' everywhere. Real grown ups, dressed in their finest, eating fancy dishes. What was I doing here?

My companion led the way to the back of the room where there was a tiny bar with four stools lined up next to it. The barman was a skinny youth in a bow tie barely older than us. My friend ordered a pint for himself and half a lager and lime for me. I gave him a look of alarm. My stare said, 'what did you get me that for? I'm not legally allowed to drink yet!'

'It's okay in a restaurant!' he whispered in response.

Soon we were sitting at a round table with a white cloth on it. The waiter lit the candle and gave us menus. I was not even slightly hungry. The starters were:

Fruit Juice
Melon
Prawn Cocktail

I ordered a pineapple juice for my starter and tried to make small talk while my friend ate his melon.

I must have not been all pineappled out because for my main course I had gammon, chips and pineapple. I could not relax and was really scared of committing some major social faux pas. I didn't recognise a lot of what was on the sweet trolley but following my pal's advice I had Black Forest gateaux. He bought me another lager and lime and we were presented with an after eight mint each and the bill, which he wouldn't let me see.

I was relieved to get home although I pretended I'd had a wonderful time. My friend came in for a while and we sat in the kitchen, smoking cigarettes lit with my new lighter. But before I sat down I ran upstairs and put on my jeans, a T shirt and my tennis shoes.

When I came back down my friend looked at me for a moment and said, 'you're a funny girl. I can't imagine what you'll be like when you're in your fifties.'

**THE END**

Contact Rain McAlistair at:

*[rainmcalistair@eircom.net](rainmcalistair@eircom.net)*
*[www.rainmcalistair.com](www.rainmcalistair.com)*

Printed in Great Britain
by Amazon